The Saber-Toothed Tiger

The Saber-Toothed Tiger

The One Reason Women Stay with Abusive Men

Josée Perrine, MA

iUniverse, Inc.
New York   Bloomington

The Saber-Toothed Tiger
The One Reason Women Stay with Abusive Men

Copyright © 2010 by Josée Perrine

All rights reserved. No part of this book may be used or reproduced by any means, graphic, electronic, or mechanical, including photocopying, recording, taping or by any information storage retrieval system without the written permission of the publisher except in the case of brief quotations embodied in critical articles and reviews.

iUniverse books may be ordered through booksellers or by contacting:

iUniverse
1663 Liberty Drive
Bloomington, IN 47403
www.iuniverse.com
1-800-Authors (1-800-288-4677)

Because of the dynamic nature of the Internet, any Web addresses or links contained in this book may have changed since publication and may no longer be valid. The views expressed in this work are solely those of the author and do not necessarily reflect the views of the publisher, and the publisher hereby disclaims any responsibility for them.

ISBN: 978-1-4502-0077-6 (sc)
ISBN: 978-1-4502-0079-0 (hc)
ISBN: 978-1-4502-0078-3 (ebook)

Printed in the United States of America

iUniverse rev. date: 01/27/10

For Jerry Michael Cinani

Contents

Acknowledgments ix
Author's Note xi
Smilodon fatalis xiii
Introduction xv
1. Same Strokes for Different Folks 1
2. It Isn't About Low Self-Esteem 10
3. It's Not About the Men 19
4. Why You Think You Stay 26
5. Sex: The Last Excuse to Stay 47
6. Preparing to Meet the Saber-Toothed Tiger 54
7. Emotional Oatmeal 59
8. The Saber-Toothed Tiger 65
9. Growing Up with the Saber-Toothed Tiger 72
10. The Value of Loneliness 78
11. Dear Old Dad 88
12. Hunger 94
13. Flat-Headed Children 102
14. Learning to Love Yourself 112
15. The Hitler Voice 118
16. Sitting With The Tiger and Fear of Freedom 124
17. Future Tense 129
18. Practice Dating and Being Healthy 132
19. Making Peace with Mom, Dad, and the Tiger ... 142

References 147

Acknowledgments

Thank you to every woman who sat with me, disclosed the secrets of her abuse, and gave me the opportunity to learn and understand the true reason why women stay with abusive men.

Thank you to Jerry Cinani and Dr. William Jenkins, my business partners and mentors, who gave me the opportunity to join them in practice and continually help me to grow in the art of counseling.

Thank you to the Board of Directors for Advocates to End Domestic Violence, and special thanks to Lisa Lee, Executive Director and her staff, for providing me a place to learn and for their ongoing support of women in need.

Author's Note

I honor the confidentiality of everyone who trusted me with their personal stories of pain and healing. The stories in this book are true; however, in order to protect each person's privacy, names have been changed and the people and details depicted are fictionalized compilations. Any similarity to a person, living or dead, or an actual event is unintended and coincidental.

Smilodon fatalis

"With their enormous, deadly-sharp canines, saber-toothed carnivores are well known to many people as frightening and ferocious predators ..." (University of California 2006, para.1). The saber-toothed tiger was not a particularly fast predator, and he most likely waited for his prey to come near before attacking from an ambush position (Shaw 2005; Illinois State Museum 2006, para.9). The structure of the bones in his throat indicates that the saber-toothed tiger could roar, and just as today's felines fight over mates, the saber-toothed tiger probably roared loudly as he fought (University of California 2006, para.6). There are differing opinions among paleontologists about how the saber-toothed tiger used his large teeth. Some think the tiger used them to seize and hold his prey, others believe the canines were "used to deliver a fatal ripping wound to the belly or throat of a prey animal" (University of California 2006, para.2). The wound would cripple the animal and the tiger would wait for his prey to die. The saber-toothed tiger must have been terrifying.

Introduction

This is a book about discovery, pain, hope, and healing. My thoughts about abusive relationships come from the many stories I have heard as a counselor working with abused women. This book describes what happens before, during, and after an abusive relationship, and what I have found to be the *one true underlying* reason why women stay in abusive relationships. Some of you may have difficulty understanding this distinct emotional experience that I call "the Saber-Toothed Tiger." Others have lived with it their entire lives. If you have been involved in an abusive relationship, you will encounter a deep fear of the tiger, but you will also feel relieved that you finally understand and know the tiger—and yourself.

I have worked mostly with women survivors of male domestic violence, but I have found that the same profile also applies to men who have been abused by women as well as lesbian women in abusive relationships. I have not worked with homosexual men, but intuitively I believe the concepts about abuse presented in this book also apply to their relationships. However, for the sake of consistency and because most abusers are male (Pence and Paymar 1993; Barnett et al. 2005; Lauer and Lauer 2007; Simons et al. 2004), abusers will be referred to as male and survivors as female.

There have been a number of arguments put forth in the past that attempt to explain why women remain in obviously dangerous relationships. One such proposition suggests that women stay in abusive relationships because they somehow become "brainwashed" into believing they deserve to be treated badly (Walker 1979). They come to believe it is their fault that the abuse is happening. The abused woman thinks if only she had cleaned the house just right like he expected, or made the soup less salty, or if she'd just lose that extra twenty pounds, then surely he would be pleased and stop criticizing her. If only she were perfect! This behavior and misguided thinking may indeed occur in an abusive relationship, but it is not the reason why women stay. It doesn't explain why a woman stays long enough for the brainwashing to occur. Many women end relationships as soon as the controlling, manipulative, or threatening behavior begins. But other women, women who end up being physically and mentally abused, stay long past the initial signs of abuse. Many stay until their lives are in danger, and some never make it out.

There are other theories to consider as well. The sex-role theory posits that women are socialized to accept the role of "victim" (Chibucos et al. 2005). Other theories propose that women are victims of "learned helplessness," lack resources and money, and have low self-esteem (Karraker and Grochowski 2006). Some women say they stay because they are afraid of abandonment, are "co-dependent," are enmeshed, lack identity, or have separation anxiety. Some women accept the notion that because they saw their mothers being beaten, then they would naturally end up in the same situation. Others blame their situation on the fact that they were sexually or physically abused as children. Murray A.. Straus, Co-Director, Family Research Laboratory, University of New Hampshire, Richard J. Gelles, Director, Center for Research onYouth and Social Policy, Penn School of Social Policy and Practice, and Suzane K. Steinmetz, Director, Family Research Centerand Professor of Sociology, Indiana University (1980) quote a social worker in a 1977 article from the *Maine Times*: "There are battered women whose fathers knocked their mothers around and who knocked them around when they were kids … the beatings were how they got their strokes. My opinion is that you tend to repeat the feeling that you had as a child … not just the behavior patterns, but you repeat experiencing a familiar feeling. Even if it's unpleasant … it's familiar." I disagree. How does this explanation account for the number of women who were raised in homes without violence? It certainly does not provide an explanation for the woman you will meet later in this book who was raised by loving parents. Although some women I have counseled experienced abuse during their childhood, most of the women who experienced domestic violence have no history of family/parental physical abuse. In addition, I think it is insulting to these women to assert that being beaten is how they "get their strokes."

Some women simply believe that they "love too much." Although some or all of these concepts may play a part in an abusive relationship, they are not the *reasons* women are attracted to, become involved with, and stay with abusive men. These beliefs and reactions occur as a *result* of the abuse, but are not the reasons women stay even after the abuse becomes extreme. These concepts do not explain a woman's initial attraction to an abusive man, or the decision to remain with him following the first incident of control or abuse.

Additionally, there are cases where these theories do not apply. There are many women who have been described as "co-dependent" in relationships where there is drug or alcohol addiction, but the women are not physically abused. And certainly, there are people who have anxiety and fear at the thought of losing their partners. But again, that doesn't equate to the acceptance of physical violence.

While doing research for this book, I reviewed Straus, Gelles, and Steinmetz's writing from 1980. At that time, Women's Liberation was somewhat new, and the authors wrote about the need to "change the sexist character of society and the family (1980, 242)." They discuss inequality in the home, and flatly state that "inequality in the home is a prime contributor to violence between family members … as long as we expect men to head the family because they are men and women to care for children because they are women, we are going to have potential conflict and violence in homes" (1980, 242). Well, it's been a long time since 1980 and the face of families has changed dramatically. Women have worked outside the home for years now. We attend college in higher numbers than ever, have far greater earning power, and have learned to balance our home, career, and social lives quite well, thank you. So why hasn't domestic violence decreased? Simply put, because inequality had little to do with it. Again, traditional families have for years defined men's and women's work differently. Some couples today prefer to return to that tradition, and it works well for them and does not increase the risk for violence. There are now, and were in the past, scores of households with clearly defined sex roles where violence never occurred. In fact, many of these families had a deep respect for one another and appreciation for knowing that one's work, whatever it was, had value. The women I see are rarely from "traditional" homes. They range from single mothers who earn more than their abusive boyfriends to successful women in their own right to wives of executives and doctors. Going to the extreme one could say all women have been victimized by paternal cultures and limited in their choices of education and employment. Regardless, all women do not tolerate abusive behavior even though they may recognize their victimization by a male-dominated society.

These attempts to explain women's behavior actually are detrimental and delay women from leaving abusive relationships. Women try to fit their experience to these theories in order to make sense of what is happening to them, and if they can explain it they believe they can change it. If it makes sense, then it is logical. It can be analyzed and corrected. In fact, these concepts are insulting and offensive to women. It places the woman in a "less than" position. Similar to the notion of "brainwashing" by the abuser, these concepts imply to a woman that there is something lacking within her and if she discovers what it is, she can correct it and the abuse will end. For instance, if she could learn to be independent, know her true identity, get over her fear of abandonment, or forget that her mother was beaten, then she would be able to leave her abuser or change the relationship so the abuse would end. But how does one go about doing this? And if she has been in counseling and worked on self-esteem and independence, but becomes involved in another abusive relationship, she becomes more confused and feels as if she is a failure who has something particularly wrong with her. Women know there has to be a reason why they find it almost impossible to leave their abusers, so they search for any explanation that might seem even vaguely appropriate.

From my years of working with women in abusive relationships, I have found only one underlying reason why women stay in abusive relationships. The more women I work with, the more I know the theories I discussed earlier are inaccurate. Instead, they should all be considered symptoms of the fundamental underlying cause. People of all ages, races, religions, geographical areas, personality types, and intellectual abilities become involved in abusive relationships—even women who function daily in work situations where they are able to direct others, confront supervisors, or take on the nasty store clerk who gave them a hard time. Women from a range of occupations and incomes—fast food servers, attorneys, and minimum wage earners to the downright rich become involved in abusive relationships. How can otherwise intelligent, functioning women allow themselves to be beaten, sometimes nearly to death, in their own homes by the men they love the most? Surely they don't change from being capable women in the world to being terrorized at home with the flick of a switch or the closing of their front doors. Yet, this is indeed what happens. If women continue to buy into the old ideas that attempt to explain why they are in abusive relationships, they will repeat their thinking and behavior and find themselves again with abusive partners. Women are able to change their lives when they become truly aware and fully understand why they stay. Only then can they make permanent and effective changes that will result in healthy relationships. After you read this book, you will know how a primary emotion plays a key role in abusive relationships. This fundamental emotion, experienced in a different way and at a deeper level, is the underlying foundation, the starting point that allows abuse.

In their comprehensive book *Family Violence in the United States* (2005), Denise Hines and Kathleen Malley-Morrison quote statistics from The U.S. Department of Justice. In 2001 there were a reported 588,490 cases of violence against women by their intimate partners. However, "these DOJ statistics reflect only the incidents of wife abuse deemed criminal behavior by the respondents." The authors discuss the difficulty of obtaining accurate information due to the different definitions used to determine what is and isn't domestic violence. Ola Barnett, Professor Emerita of Psychology, Pepperdine University, Clinical Psychologist Cindy Miller-Perrine, and Sociologist, Robin Perrin (2005) also address this issue, "According to an FBI report, of the 13,752 homicides reported in the United States in 2001, 2,387 (17%) were committed by family members, boyfriends, or girlfriends of the victims." They note that in about half of all homicides the assailant is not known and therefore, the actual percentage of murders within families is most likely much higher, "well over 20%." They further state, "women are especially vulnerable within the family" and according to Callie Marie Rennison, Department of Criminology and Criminal Justice, University of Missouri, (2001), "women make up approximately three-quarters of all victims of intimate homicide ... nearly one-third (32%) of female homicide victims in 2001 were killed by intimates (i.e., husbands, ex-husbands, boyfriends, or ex-boyfriends)." More frightening is when they say "once again, it should be noted that the actual proportion is probably considerably higher, given that so many homicides go unsolved" (U.S. Department of Justice 2002). "It is not unreasonable to speculate that the proportion of female homicide victims who are killed by intimates or other family members may be as high as 50%, a figure that is consistent with historical evidence on intimate homicide" (Dobash and Dobash 1979). It has been my experience working with victims of domestic violence that many incidences are not reported, and I have personally witnessed police reports in which initial charges of domestic battery against perpetrators have been reduced to disturbing the peace.

Over the past years, there has been increased discussion and awareness of what constitutes domestic violence (Barnett et al. 2005; Hines and Malley-Morrison 2005; Ihinger-Tallman and Cooney 2005; Price et al. 2000). Some abuse is verbal—name-calling, insults to women and their families, put-downs, sarcasm. Physical abuse too is well known—restraining movement, pulling hair, pinching, slapping, pushing, punching, twisting arms or fingers, breaking bones, burning, stabbing, shooting, and rape. I have heard too many stories of abuse from women like Belinda, pregnant with her first child, whose fiancé threw her off a balcony, followed her as she tried to crawl to safety and beat her with a bat until she miscarried the only child she will ever have. Tiffany's boyfriend used a cigarette to burn her genitals. Nora's husband slashed her with a knife while their three-year-old daughter watched. These women arrived in counseling as victims of domestic violence, but they left as survivors—they courageously told their stories, learned why they remained with their abusers, looked at their own reflections in the mirror, faced guilt and shame, accepted the reality of their lives, and worked hard to accomplish change.

There are many more women who did not endure that degree of violence, but who were nonetheless assaulted physically, verbally, or psychologically. There is always a mountain of emotional and psychological pain that accompanies abuse of any kind. Women often tell me the emotional abuse is worse than any physical pain they have endured. This makes sense when you understand the underlying emotional state that makes women vulnerable and leads to abusive relationships. According to Hines and Malley-Morrison (2005), reports of domestic violence against women are dropping. I truly hope this is because there actually are fewer acts of violence and that the trend continues until abuse no longer occurs. I believe when women have an understanding of their emotional history and why they remain in abusive relationships, they will have the tools they need to leave and never become involved in another again. Additionally, if young women are aware of the emotional condition that leads to abusive relationships, they will be able to avoid them. There will be a significant reduction in abuse if women learn the critical emotional need that drives them to enter into and stay in abusive relationships. It is my sincerest hope that this book will make that difference in women's lives.

Alice and Melody come from different backgrounds, but they share a similarity that results in common pain and tragedy. They are only two of hundreds of women I have counseled. Some of these women attended counseling for only a short period of time, while others saw it through to the end. I can tell you that the women who stay in counseling until they have experienced each step of therapy are the ones who gain the greatest degree of self-awareness, a true understanding of why they were attracted to their abusers, and why they stayed after the abuse began. They are the most able to make significant changes in their lives. Each woman's story is different, but they all share the same underlying theme. It's this shared theme that led me to develop a counseling method that addresses the definitive reason why women stay with their abusers or repeatedly connect with abusive men.

If you are in an abusive relationship, whether verbal, psychological, or physical, or if you have left one and want to discover why you stayed so long, this book will guide you to understanding and change. If you have repeatedly ended up in abusive relationships, *The Saber-Toothed Tiger* will put you on a life-changing path. I wrote this book for every woman who knows she should leave but finds it impossible to follow through, or who has left and wants to make sure her next relationship is not with an abusive man. *The Saber-Toothed Tiger* will explain how a profound feeling, loneliness, drives you toward abusive relationships. Loneliness in this sense, however, is different than the lonely feelings other women experience. The "saber-toothed tiger" is unrelenting and pervasive. This book will help you understand your past and find a way to live beyond this loneliness.

1

Same Strokes for Different Folks

Alice arrived at my evening support group for battered women. She had attended several meetings in the past and usually sat quietly, listening to the other women relate the events that led them to seek help. It was a cool fall evening, but not cold enough to explain why Alice was bundled in a heavy blanket and boots. It looked as if she needed to protect herself, and the blanket provided a sense of safety and security. She snuggled into one of the overstuffed chairs and immediately grabbed a few tissues, an indication that tonight she was ready to tell her story. She started with the story of her first marriage.

"I was so ready to leave home! My parents were very strict. I had to go to church three times a week and there were so many rules. My mother always questioned me about boys and whether I was behaving like a good girl. I felt like I was being watched all the time. As soon as I was eighteen, I was ready to get out. I met my first husband in church. He was a little bit older than me and had been in the army—he had a good income so I thought what the heck, might as well get married and have a life of my own." Alice laughed out loud at how naïve she had been. The other women in the group nodded sympathetically, as many had experienced something similar.

Alice continued, "Boy, was I wrong. At first he seemed nice, but he turned out to be just like my father. He controlled everything I did. If I didn't do something just the way he wanted, he would call me stupid and say things like 'didn't your parents teach you anything?' and 'didn't you learn anything in school?' I felt like I was right back home again. I stayed as long as I could, but it just got to be too much." Her voice quieted, and looking at the floor, Alice revealed how she finally got out of her marriage.

"I knew the only way I could leave was to have an affair. That's the only reason the church would allow my husband to divorce me. I know this sounds awful, and I'm not too proud of it, but I made a plan and actually looked for someone to cheat with. He was just some guy I met at work, a delivery guy. He seemed like he was looking for someone, so I went for it. It was a one-time thing, enough to get me branded with the big scarlet letter, and it worked! But you know what? When I told my husband, he acted like he expected me to do that, like I was a typical loose woman. That still hurts. I wasn't a bad person. I just couldn't figure another way out."

Alice's face brightened when she described what happened next. "I was so glad to be gone from my family and husband. I found a good job in a city about five hundred miles away. Whew, finally freedom! I had a great time partying with my girlfriends, but I always felt like something was missing. Then I met Randy and my world got rocked! I fell in love hard. He swept me off my feet. He was fun, seemed like he didn't have a care in the world, and liked to have a good time. We got married a month after we met and I was so happy. I felt like something I had waited for all my life had finally happened."

A sad and confused look swept over Alice's face. She looked as if she still could not understand how that happiness had changed to something so different and frightening. "It seemed like Randy really loved me. He would get so angry if any man looked at me, and I thought he just loved me so much. If he didn't like my hair, I changed it. If he said he wanted chicken for dinner, I was off to the store. I'd do anything for him, but it got to be like he seemed angry at me all the time. Nothing I tried seemed to make him happy. I knew he liked to party before we met, and he kept drinking and sometimes he'd use drugs. I thought maybe if I did drugs with him, he'd stay home more and want to be with me, 'cause he would go out with his friends to do drugs. So I did some drugs and drank, but then I found out I was pregnant. I thought that would really straighten us both out, but we kept using. I wanted the baby, and he said he wanted a family, but when I was four months along, he started getting mean. He started being physical with me, slapping and punching me if I ever complained. Sometimes I didn't even know why he was angry."

Alice started to cry as she recalled how things unraveled when it should have been the happiest time of her life. "He called me a whore and said the baby probably wasn't even his. I couldn't believe that! I loved him so much. I never would have cheated on him. I never wanted to lose him. I thought maybe my being pregnant was too stressful for him. When I had little Joey, it was wonderful. He was so cute. I thought Randy would melt like I did when he saw Joey. But he didn't change, he got worse. I think he started cheating on me, too. I started doing drugs again so maybe he'd stay home. I went back to work. Randy didn't have a job anymore, and he wouldn't stay with Joey."

Alice's life continued to be ruled by drugs and violence, but she didn't leave. She continued to love Randy even though his behavior was deplorable. She told us, "It got so bad over the years, we started injecting together. Let me tell you how dumb I am. I can't stand needles, so Randy would put the needle in for me. I thought that showed he still loved me. And then we'd smoke pot to come down. Neither of us could keep a job anymore. It was awful! We didn't have any furniture, and we lived in this little dirty motel room. Joey hardly ever went to school. Poor Joey, he saw me getting punched around all the time. It was just us, no relatives and no friends, no one in our lives but other drug users. Time went by and we just kept at it."

Alice started to cry harder, wiping her tears with the back of her hands, shame written all over her face. "Twelve years!

I can't believe I did this to my son. He started using too—Randy gave it to him! Now he's in rehab. He can't even read good, and the social worker says he has learning disabilities because I was using when I was pregnant. And now I'm sick. I got hepatitis C from the needles." Alice looked incredulous. "Twelve years! I loved him, but when he started hitting Joey too, I decided I had to leave. And now Joey acts just like his dad, calling me names and breaking my things. He won't listen to me at all. What's wrong with me? I still love Randy. It doesn't make sense!"

Although Alice couldn't leave when her husband abused her, the love for her son motivated her to try to change her life. She summoned all her courage, took her son, and moved into a shelter. It would be easy to blame Randy's drug use for his violence toward Alice and Joey. And we could say Alice stayed because she too became addicted. But there are plenty of relationships that include addiction that are not violent. And there are also plenty of abusive men who aren't addicted to drugs and as many women who stay with them. Often, physical abuse begins when a woman becomes pregnant. According to the March of Dimes Birth Defects Foundation, 25 to 45 percent of all women who are battered are abused during pregnancy. Certainly, we wouldn't say that pregnancy causes violence. The same logic applies to drug or alcohol addiction and its relationship to domestic violence. Although violence can occur in a relationship where there is substance abuse or addiction, it is not the cause of ongoing violence toward a partner. Nevertheless, some men will use their substance abuse as an excuse for their violent behavior, and some women will risk their own lives and the lives of their unborn babies for something much more addictive than drugs.

Melody's Story

Melody began attending group about the same time as Alice. She was tall and slim with long straight black hair and warm dark eyes. Her angular body belied a softness that others felt when they were around her. She reminded me of a kindly aunt who would bake cookies and patiently listen to my troubles. Melody shared her story.

"I've been married for over thirty years. We have four children; two are grown and have their own lives. Our families have been here for years; we can trace our roots back over a hundred years, right here in this area. My husband and I have a good business. I do the books and sales, and he does the building and warranties. Neither of us drinks or does drugs. We look like the perfect family, don't we? People will never believe what has been going on. I'm moving into a shelter, and I don't think anyone will understand. I told my older kids, and they are already angry with me. They say I've stayed with my husband this long, I should keep quiet and not embarrass the family."

It's true that to the outside world, Melody's family looked secure and stable. However, as is often the case with dysfunctional families, one of Melody's kids began acting out. Her eleven-year-old son almost died from a drug overdose. His behavior was the only visible indication that something was very wrong in the family. Like Alice, Melody endured physical and emotional abuse from her husband throughout her marriage and didn't leave until her son also became a victim. Despite the loss of her family, Melody knew she had to save herself and at least the youngest of her children, even if no one believed her story. There were many times throughout the counseling process when Melody knew it would be easier to return to her husband, particularly when she barely had enough money to buy groceries. But as she began to understand why she had stayed in the abusive relationship and what she needed to do to change, she grew determined to gain her freedom from her husband, the abuse, and her past.

It is rare for a woman to go to a shelter the first time she experiences abuse. The first act of violence is shocking, but you dismiss it as an aberration. The man who says he loves you can't really be hurting you. Leaving your home or going to a shelter is usually a last resort and a desperate act that you hope will be a wake-up call to your abuser. Perhaps you went to a shelter or to a friend's house hoping that if you showed your partner you were serious about leaving, he would change. Alice, Melody, and virtually all the other women I've counseled thought the same thing. They hoped that after they left their partners the men would realize how awful life would be without them. Maybe you hoped your partner would tell you how sorry he was and that he can't live without you. After all, that's how *you* felt about leaving. Don't men feel the same way? Leaving someone you love that much is nearly impossible, and you believe your man loves you, otherwise why would he have behaved so jealously?

Inga's Terror

Inga was thirty-four years old and had been with her abuser for seven years. I met her on a summer afternoon, and as I looked at her sitting on the couch in the shelter's office, I could see that at one time she had been beautiful. But now there was a strained look about her, and I could see scars on her chin and forehead. Her blonde hair fell loosely over her shoulders, and she wore just the right amount of eye makeup to attract my gaze to that part of her face. She held her mouth almost closed when she talked, and the reason became evident as she told me her story. Over the years of abuse her boyfriend had knocked out or broken most of her teeth, and the remaining teeth had shifted from their original positions, giving her mouth a distorted appearance. She told me about the time he had pushed her from a moving car, blackened her eyes with his fists, and broken her fingers. The latest abuse followed a minor disagreement about car insurance. Inga related the story in a matter-of-fact way, as if it were a script she had memorized. She did not cry or seem sad. Nor did she seem in shock, although her story is certainly shocking.

"My boyfriend locked me in the bedroom, and I could hear him outside the door, fumbling around with something. Then he started screaming at me, cursing, calling me horrible names. I heard the doorknob turn, it creaked a little, and then he came through the door like a bull. He had a can of lighter fluid, the kind you use on the barbeque, and he started spraying it around the room and on me and the bed. I couldn't even think. It was all like in slow motion. He was yelling something about killing me or burning me up, and how no one would ever want me again. I'd be all scarred up. I saw him take the lighter and throw it on the bed. Everything was going slower and slower. I don't know how, but I jumped up and headed for the window. Somehow I went through the glass and landed in the yard. The neighbors were outside by that time and called the police. In the hospital they fixed my broken collarbone and all the cuts. He went to jail. This time I'm not going back. My boss is going to help me with a place to live and pay the doctor bills. He's good people."

As I listened, trying not to see the images that formed in my mind and knowing where I needed to lead her in the process of healing, I already knew we would not finish our work. I knew she would stay long enough to hear what she did not want to know, and she was not ready to do the hard work that needed to be done. I can tell within the first few minutes of listening to a woman whether she is attempting to get her abuser's attention or she's ready to leave for good. How a woman tells what has happened to her lets me know where she is in the process of change. If a woman tells her story of loss without emotional expression and anguish, and with an "I'll show him" attitude, I know it's another story that is only half told. She's going back. Inga was still trying to teach her boyfriend a lesson. A few weeks after our meeting, she contacted him and he cried, he apologized, and he promised never again. Inga believed, she hoped, she forgave, she loved and returned to the man who tried to kill her, and eventually he did. Abusers *know* when a woman will come back no matter how bad it gets.

If you leave your abuser in an effort to get his attention, his reaction might be different from Inga's boyfriend. You may move out with the same hope that your abuser will "get it" and change, but he may do nothing to encourage your return. He may be cold and not try to locate you. It may seem as if he doesn't care. Maybe he will spend your savings on toys for himself. He might go out and have sex with someone you know. Maybe he'll even move another woman into your home and have sex in your bed. When you hear about his behavior, and he will ensure that somehow you do, you'll probably feel like you've made a mistake. The threat of losing the relationship is too great a risk and you have to return. You have to prove to yourself that your man loves you, otherwise why would you tolerate the abuse? There has to be a reason. He *has* to love you. Since there is another woman involved, you now have someone else to blame for your pain. You shift the focus of your anger, pain, and sorrow from its true source, your abuser, to someone outside the relationship—the other woman. This allows you to stay connected to your abuser. Your abuser also knows that his behavior will motivate you to return. On some level he knows there is something more threatening than infidelity or loss of dignity that will keep you with him. You both know if you come home, the other woman will leave and your abuser will do nothing to stop her. The "other woman" is just a pawn the abusive man uses to manipulate his victim. But you will interpret this behavior as proof of his love for you. When he sees how much you love him by forgiving *even this*, he will have to love you more! So you go home. And nothing changes.

It is estimated that women return to abusive relationships an average of seven to twelve times. I don't know if that's true, but there certainly have been women in my groups who have returned so many times they've lost count. I can't recall anyone saying, "Yep, he hit me just once and I was out of there!" Women who are able to leave the first time they experience abuse, or even come close to it, don't need counseling. They don't end up in shelters. If someone hits them or calls them names, they leave, tell all their friends what an ass he is, and never look back. What is the difference between women who don't tolerate abuse in *any* form, and women who endure *every* abuse?

2

It Isn't About Low Self-Esteem

Self-esteem: "belief in oneself; self-respect." —*Webster New World College Dictionary*

Janet was twenty-three years old and engaged to Charles. They dated for two years before becoming engaged, and they shared similar tastes in music and poetry. He was intelligent, hardworking, and was about to graduate from college with a degree in engineering.

Janet held a well-paying clerical job with a national company. She traveled, attended evening college classes, and spent plenty of money and time on herself. Janet and Charles had disagreements that were resolved by compromise or agreeing to disagree, and there was never a hint of possessiveness or violence. The relationship was comfortable, intellectually stimulating, and fun, but Janet felt something was missing. She loved Charles, and he met all the standards she had set for herself about men. Intellectually, she knew Charles had the characteristics that make a man a good husband, yet Janet always felt that somehow the relationship was incomplete. While dating Charles, Janet met Darren, a man very different from Charles. She ended the relationship with Charles and quickly married Darren.

Janet came to counseling six months after her divorce from Darren. They had been married twenty years and there was no physical violence until the last five years of the marriage. She initiated counseling in order to try to make sense of what had happened to her and her marriage.

Janet's soft Southern accent lent a particular charm to her story. "I was going to marry Charles, but then I met Darren. Have you seen that movie *Grease*, where the couple meets in the summer and falls in love? That's what it was like for Darren and me. I was on vacation and I met him at the beach."

She laughed, perhaps thinking about how clichéd her story sounded. "I remember the first time I saw him standing there with his buddies. I felt like I had known him my whole life. It was magic! All I had to do was smile, and he came over and talked and talked. He had such a sense of humor and was so smart and gentlemanly. He was very sure of himself with women. I wasn't used to that. He wrote poetry, too. I just die for poetry and flowers. After I went home from vacation, I just couldn't stop thinking about him. I had to find a way to see him again! I started writing to him, and he talked about wanting a woman to be his queen. Wow, I loved that, 'cause I was an old-fashioned girl."

Of course, Janet didn't realize that if she were to be queen, then Darren would be king, which meant that he would have the power and authority. Nevertheless, at the time it sounded like a dream.

"We kept writing and one day Darren said he would be coming to my city and asked would I marry him if he came. I thought I had died and gone to heaven! I broke up with Charles in five minutes!" Janet laughed heartily. "I put a wedding together faster than you can say it. I loved that man for twenty years no matter what, and there were a lot of 'whats' along the way."

Janet and Darren married, moved to his hometown, and within a few years they had two children, a girl and a boy, just like they had planned. They bought a home in a working-class neighborhood. Janet was active in every school function and volunteered time for community fundraisers while Darren held a government job and finished his college education. Janet had always wanted an education, but Darren just wasn't good with money. He had military financial assistance for school, and Janet didn't have any way to pay for school for herself, but she gladly sacrificed her dream so her husband could get a degree. She loved her husband deeply and wanted to support him. Janet believed his education would benefit the family financially as well as set an example of achievement for their children.

Over the next few months of counseling, Janet continued the history of her marriage and began to piece together the subtle clues that indicated things were not as magical as they first appeared. "I wanted to be perfect for Darren. I'd sit on the front porch waiting for him to come home from work. I'd be wearing a dress he liked, have my makeup on, the house would be spotless. I didn't want to be doing housework when he was around. I just wanted to spend every minute with him. I knew just what he liked me to wear. His eyes would light up when he saw me." Janet's face darkened as she recalled how she came to know just what he liked.

"When we were first married, I moved all my clothes into the apartment we rented and unpacked them. I was proud of my clothes. I had a good job before I was married, and I had professional-looking, expensive suits and dresses. Darren came from a different background and said that I had 'drab-colored' clothes. He made fun of my job, saying I was a 'diminutive little secretary.' It didn't occur to him, or now that I look back on it, maybe it *did* occur to him, that I made more money than he did. But, you know, I was young and I thought a man who had been around as much as he had would know about what made a woman attractive. So I listened and started wearing the kind of things he liked. I wanted to make him happy."

Janet and I discussed how her self-esteem had changed over the years of marriage. "I believed I had the best marriage. Darren and I never fought. We had maybe two disagreements in twenty years. Now that I look back on that, it might have told me something more, but I thought it was a good thing, like it meant we really loved each other. I knew I could take care of a household, had a job I loved, spent quality time with my children, and gave to the community and church. I had good self-esteem. I cared about how I looked, my house was clean and neat, and I'm an incredibly organized person. I knew I was intelligent, too. I read a lot of books. People could tell by looking at me that I had self-respect. I took care of myself. I always looked good. I can see now how it was. I did real well at work and such, but with Darren, I just folded in. I never wanted to lose him so I did whatever he wanted. He was always jealous and I didn't mind at first, but you know, you get older and it doesn't make sense anymore. Something changed in him. He got mean and violent. I kept trying to make it go back to the way it was, but it got worse and worse. I was in control and doing well in every aspect of my life, except at home. My family was falling apart, and worst of all, I had lost myself."

Where did it go wrong for Janet? How could her belief in herself vanish so quickly when Darren hurled a vase across the room, glancing off her temple, leaving her bruised and cut? She had fifteen years without violence. She didn't start out as a victim. She believed in herself. She believed in Darren. If anybody else in the world had treated Janet that way, he or she would be in jail. There are plenty of examples from those many years where she stood up for herself! So why didn't that self-esteem propel her right out the door? Why didn't that self-esteem exist in her marital relationship? Why did Janet stay when the abuse escalated—she was choked, kicked, punched, bound, and slashed with a knife, bruised and bleeding—for five more years?

At the end of those five years, it was true that Janet didn't have much self-esteem or self-respect left *within the relationship*. But that doesn't mean she didn't have it before. Recall that Janet had evident self-esteem within her relationship with Charles. It could be described as a healthy relationship, one that might have resulted in marriage, children, and fulfillment of individual and mutual goals. Janet chose to marry Darren instead of Charles for a reason and it had nothing to do with self-esteem. She began to lose her self-esteem within the relationship the day she married Darren, and it continued to decrease as she stayed in the relationship and allowed the criticism and eventual brutality and isolation to continue. Janet's self-esteem didn't vanish with one smack to the head. It faded gradually, one put-down at a time.

In contrast, and at the same time, her self-esteem *outside* the relationship increased. Janet returned to college, maintained a rewarding job, and received daily compliments from her supervisors and co-workers. She was well aware of her ability, intelligence, and accomplishments. She believed in herself and was accurate in her assessment of her self-efficacy—outside of the relationship.

Successful Women, Self-Esteem, and Abuse

Surely women who are able to graduate college and build careers believe in themselves and have demonstrated that belief through achieving personal and career goals. Think of several actresses and celebrities you have heard of who reported being abused, yet returned to their partners or became involved with the next abusive man. There are plenty of women who have brains, beauty, and success who have proven their belief in themselves, and their abilities yet end up in abusive relationships. In the outside world, they demonstrate respect for themselves and there is evidence they care about, and for, themselves. Why aren't these characteristics evident at home?

Often, it is the successful, achieving woman who has the most difficulty making sense of her situation. At work she is rewarded for her ability and competence, and she receives regular positive feedback. Her "outside" life becomes incongruent with her home life. The abuse makes it impossible for her to explain what is happening and others cannot understand. It appears self-esteem is dimensional, and one's self-esteem can differ from one area of life to another. It's easy to say women stay in abusive relationships because of low self-esteem, but their lives deserve closer examination and explanation.

Within the abusive relationship, self-esteem certainly becomes diminished as the relationship progresses, but it is not the basis for, nor the reason why women enter into and *stay* in abusive relationships. Women often enter an abusive relationship with plenty of self-esteem and maintain it in areas outside the primary relationship, but within the relationship and in regard to being loved, their self-esteem is damaged. An abusive partner's behavior serves to undermine and destroy it.

After the initial shock of being hit, Janet quickly rationalized Darren's behavior and stuffed the memory of the incident in a dark drawer in her mind. Even after the abuse became blatant and the children were aware, it all went into the drawer. There were two years in which the only memories she had were her son's wedding and her first grandchild being born. For Janet there was something more frightening than torture.

Can you imagine—something worse than torture? It's true. I hear it all the time. Women come to group and tell horrible stories. Some sound almost ordinary, the usual hitting, shoving, and name-calling. There are other nights when I drive home craving disbelief because the story I've just heard can't be what one human being does to another under the guise of love. We understand hate. We are able to comprehend a despot who tortures people because he despises them. He never said he loved them. He never promised to love and cherish. There is an absurd distortion of emotion and reality that women experience in an abusive relationship. You can see how abuse from a man who says he loves you can be automatically denied. When abuse becomes life-threatening, as in the stories of Alice and Melody, or the children are put in danger, then women can become motivated to leave. Sadly, sometimes women and children die in denial of abuse. Outside of death, the most abhorrent reaction to abuse is when a woman sacrifices her children to the beatings in order to gain the continued attention from the abuser. In order to keep their relationships, some women will even pimp their children to their abusers, allowing their children to be sexually abused. I know this does not sound logical, and to someone who has not been in this situation, it will be almost impossible to believe. This is evidence of the fear these women experience—not of their abusers, but of something more terrifying and unknown even to themselves.

Why Men Abuse Women

There are different theories about why men abuse women, and I will discuss these briefly. I don't think it wise to dwell too long on this subject, because I know how abused women think. If you have experienced abuse, you've probably spent a good deal of time trying to figure out what makes your partner behave violently toward you. If you could just discover the magic cure, you could change him and everything would be wonderful. I strongly caution you not to become involved in this kind of self-delusion. Regardless of how well you understand your partner's behavior, you are not going to change him. It's not about your man, it's about you.

If you insist on gaining more information about abusers, there are certainly plenty of books available. I provide only the briefest of information about some of the work that has been done and only to give you a glimpse of how domestic violence studies continue to focus on the men. Neil Jacobson, Professor of Psychology at the University of Washington, and John Gottman, author and founder of the Gottman Institute (1998), identified characteristics and behaviors of abusive men and determined two distinct types of batterers. They gave them catchy names, pit bulls and cobras. Along with the descriptive names for male abusers, there is a name for the chain of events that lead to violence toward one's partner. The "Cycle of Violence" describes three phases: violence, remorse, and preparation to repeat the cycle (Walker 1979). This cycle is defined strictly by the man's behavior. No one has developed catchy names for a woman's cycle of torment and fear and until now, no one has determined why women keep forgiving these brutes and agree to have their children!

Over the past twenty years, many states have passed laws ordering abusers convicted of domestic violence, both male and female, to attend domestic violence treatment programs. The treatment programs with which I am familiar are based on work with males, and when the woman is the batterer, the programs are only somewhat altered. For example, in women's classes, there is more emphasis on feelings and the role that emotions play in a woman's behavior. Women are generally perceived as responding in kind to initial violence by their partners (Lauer and Lauer 2007). Again, no catchy names for the women offenders, other than the ubiquitous "bitch" accorded to every woman at some time in her life, and sometimes regrettably, even by herself.

In addition to catchy names and treatment programs, there seem to be plenty of theories about how men become abusers (Simons et al. 2004; Pence and Paymar 1993; Ihinger-Tallman and Cooney 2005). These include public shaming by adults at critical periods in life; learned behavior while watching a father abuse a mother; religious and political privilege (submit to your husband, etc.); alcohol and/or drug abuse; anger resulting from childhood abuse; and my all-time favorite, feeling powerless because women are now in the workplace, making money and working in supervisory positions. In other words—women's equality. If you feel you need to learn more about the theories of male marital violence, I recommend reading chapter eight in *Families, Delinquency, and Crime* by Professors of Sociology Ronald Simons, Leslie Simons, and Lora Wallace (2004). However, for those of you trying to understand why you are in a violent relationship, I cannot stress enough how important it is to learn about you. You have spent far too much time already trying to make sense of what is happening in your relationship. Don't postpone your future by remaining focused on your partner.

My point here, besides providing brief information about the state of domestic violence and treatment programs in this country, is that it's still about the men. What about the women? Although a woman's self-esteem shrinks as the abusive relationship continues, it is not the reason why women stay with abusers. The incongruence between levels of self-esteem within and outside of the relationship disproves the concept that lack of self-esteem is the reason women stay with their abusers. If women know why they stay, they can learn how to leave, each and every one, and the men will stop the violence. The first act of violence against a woman will be the last because she will leave *the very first time violence occurs*. Women will stop unwittingly colluding with their abusers.

3

It's Not About the Men

The executive director of the National Network to End Domestic Violence states, "We have always looked at the victim and said, 'Well, why doesn't she just leave?' ... Everyone asks why she continues to stay; no one thinks to ask, 'Why does he hit her in the first place?'" (Feinberg in Gilbert 2007). This statement is simply not true. As I mentioned earlier, there are numerous studies, books, and articles that discuss the reasons behind men's abusive behavior. The focus has naturally gone in that direction because when the question "Why does she stay?" is asked, there has never been an adequate answer—until now.

Remember Pogo? If you're over age fifty, you might. The cartoonist Walt Kelly created a politically-aware little swamp creature named Pogo in the 1940s. In the late 1960s, Pogo made the now-famous comment, "We have met the enemy, and he is us." This is true about domestic violence as well. Men are not entirely the enemy. Am I saying women are to blame for their abuse? Not exactly. Men are responsible for their violence and there is no excuse for it. They should be held morally and legally responsible. Domestic violence should not be treated differently than any assault from a stranger—there should be fines, restitution, and depending on the severity of the assault, a prison sentence. Likewise, when women become the victims of abuse from their partners, it is their responsibility to leave, immediately and permanently. If a stranger assaulted you, would you move in with him and have his children? Of course not. Assault is assault, violence is violence, pain is pain. The same behavior merits the same response—you must end it. Don't allow it to be repeated. As I said earlier, if women left after the initial controlling, demanding, and jealous behavior, domestic violence would end, or at least be a one-time occurrence. However, as we know from countless reports, women don't leave. Instead, they return over and over again until all the theories fit.

I don't care for theories that make women the victims and imply they can't make decisions or don't know about resources. "Lack of economic alternatives is one of the three main factors which Gelles" (1976) "found associated with beaten wives remaining with their husbands" (Straus et al 1980, 207). Note the antiquity of that quote and recall my earlier discussion about women's financial status today. Yet, this outdated thinking continues to persist and women themselves adopt it as an explanation for their predicament. Remember, we're talking about women who may have successful careers, are well educated, and know what is available to them in the world. Of course, some battered women don't have large incomes, or are young and just beginning to enter the job market and may not have as much knowledge and ability as older women. However, it's doubtful there is anyone who hasn't heard of food stamps, welfare, child care assistance, low-income housing, and various other programs available to those in need. Some women may not know exactly how to access these programs, but they know the resources exist. With effort, they can find help, and it is insulting to imply that because someone is young or poor, they are incapable of finding help. My experience has actually been the opposite. Despite poverty, disability, or any other obstacle, women have survived thanks to their ability to find and effectively manage the resources needed to feed, clothe, and shelter their families. Abused women don't need further patronization from those who want to pigeonhole them as victims or who can't find a more significant reason why someone would want to stay with an abuser. Believing that abused women are simply not too bright to leave is a lot easier than facing the fact that very smart women are abused and stay with their abusers. Based on the outdated explanations I presented earlier, it is hard to accept that smart, capable women choose to stay in violent relationships. But that is exactly what happens. They may not be consciously aware of it, but they choose the abuser and they choose to stay, and it makes perfect sense when they learn the truth.

I have discovered that regardless of age, income, intellect, or ability, it is the same underlying need that attracts women to abusive men and the glue that holds women in the relationships. And it has nothing to do with the men, except that women keep picking the same type of man. The same reason that drives a woman into her first abusive relationship moves her into the second and third or more.

Outdated Theories

In the 1960s, a theory called "learned helplessness" was introduced (Overmier and Seligman 1967). Experiments demonstrated that when electric shocks were given to dogs, initially the animals would try to avoid or escape from the stimulus. However, after repeated exposures to shocks and with no way to avoid them, the dogs eventually gave up trying to escape. Additionally, even after being provided with a way to avoid the pain, the dogs no longer tried to escape. Later studies discussed how this theory might apply to humans (Abramson, et al 1978; Hiroto and Seligman 1975; Roth 1980). Ola Barnett, Cindy Miller-Perrin, and Robin Perrin (2005) quote J.R. Gerow's definition of learned helplessness as it relates to abused women, "a condition in which a subject does not attempt to escape from a painful or noxious situation after learning in a previous, similar situation that escape is not possible." The authors also discuss the work of Lenore Walker, who "popularized learned helplessness theory as an explanation of battered women's failure to emancipate themselves from their abusers" (2005, 288). The authors provide excellent arguments for and against Walker's theory. I come down firmly in the "against" column and will state unequivocally that abused women don't "learn helplessness." If the "learned helplessness" theory were correct, an abused woman would never be able to leave the *first* abusive relationship without outside intervention. And yet, I know many women who stayed in the first relationship for a long time and eventually and without assistance left, then became involved with another abuser, left him, and the cycle continued. It might have been extremely difficult for the women to leave, but it was not because they did not see an escape. The very fact that women *do* leave abusive relationships disproves the learned helplessness theory. And having heard all these theories about themselves and their behavior, these women still end up in my battered women's group trying to figure it out.

Abused women are often able to leave work situations where they are not treated well, but they fail to transfer this ability to romantic relationships. There is something else going on here. Women are out there in the world working diligently—there is nothing "helpless" about these women. Abused women certainly do not use the word "helpless" to describe themselves. Often they are the breadwinners in the family. They may be working single mothers or women receiving assistance from welfare. Or they may be women who own their own businesses or are even seen on the covers of popular magazines. Regardless, they have not "learned helplessness." If anything, they have "learned capability." They have learned to persevere in their public lives despite the emotional turmoil and pain in their private lives. What they have not learned is why they are in the situation they are in. That is what you will learn here.

Getting Started

When a woman first comes to group, she tells her story of abuse, sometimes very reluctantly and with many tears. As the counselor, I encourage women to share their stories in order to learn that they are not the only people to have endured the pain, humiliation, fear, and embarrassment of living in a violent situation. However, before we begin a session, I inform the women that my groups are "working groups." That means it is assumed they are in group because they want to change their situations. I inform them that this group is going to be different from other counseling they may have experienced. They will be expected to work hard at changing themselves, to look squarely in the mirror and dig deep inside themselves in order to begin the difficult journey. There are rules in group and it will be helpful for you to apply these rules to your life as well. The first rule is no Kleenex pushing. You can cry; indeed, crying is entirely appropriate and encouraged. When someone dies, we cry, we mourn. Your relationship, your family, your dreams, and your hopes died when you left the person you loved. It is time to mourn and weep, to feel pity for yourself and your children. Crying is honesty and honesty is very important now. However, the same rule applies to you as it does to the women in group—when you cry you must get your own tissues. If you mourn with your family or friends, and you know you will be crying, tell them they can not give you the Kleenex—you need to cry. You've probably already spent most of your life caring for others, particularly your abuser. Now you will begin to take care of yourself, and you will begin by wiping your own tears.

The second rule: you can't beat yourself up. You can say, "I *did* something really stupid." But you can't say, "*I'm* really stupid." Your behavior reflects something about who you are, but it is not all you are. There are plenty of people in the world who will stand in line to verbally beat you up. You can't be one of them.

Third rule—speak from an "I" position. You must change your language, and this will take some practice. You are probably accustomed to saying things like "He makes me feel so angry," or "When you try to talk and he just keeps pushing you." From now on there has to be an "**I**," bold and capitalized! Take the "he" out of the sentence and say "*I get so angry when I'm pushed*" or "*I feel so angry/hurt/betrayed when* (fill in the blank)." You cannot remove yourself from you own life. By changing your language and reinserting yourself into your speech, you will learn to be responsible for your feelings and behavior. More importantly, the change in wording changes the emphasis from other to self. When you make him responsible for how you feel, you continue to give him power over you. Take back your power!

The fourth rule: no rescuing. When appropriate, my style of counseling is to challenge a person's thinking and feelings, and at times women cry, especially when we are getting to some hard truths. When emotion becomes uncomfortable, other members often interject comforting words like, "It will be okay. Your children will always love you," or "You're beautiful on the inside." Your family and friends also might use similar words to try to rescue you from the reality of your situation. Thank them, but stop them from going any further. It is not up to your children or anyone else to make your future "okay." It is up to you. You are responsible for making changes. You have a choice. Face reality the way it is, with all of the pain, but also all the awareness that provides a means to change, or live in a delusion of love accompanied by fear, violence, death of the soul, and possibly physical death. No one is coming to rescue you! Even if they try, don't let them! If you want to learn, you will have to do the work yourself.

In addition to these rules, which are common counseling techniques, I have one final rule—we will not discuss the men.

The Saber-Toothed Tiger

When women first come to group, they often keep trying to talk about the men, just like you might be doing with anyone who will listen to you. Maybe you think that it will help you understand him and discover how he could possibly act the way he does. If you can understand then you can go home again and fix it. This time you will do it right and there will be no more violence. You will know the secret to taming him, making him happy, and making him love you—without the pain. Perhaps when you picked up this book you expected to discover what you are doing wrong. You will indeed find out what you are doing wrong, but it has nothing to do with him. You will be looking in the mirror. Some women really resent it when I say we will be looking at ourselves. They say, "We're the victims, damn it!"

When a new woman comes to my group she is allowed to share her history of abuse, but only for the purpose of joining with other group members to discover she is not alone in her sorrow. Long-time group members sometimes just dismiss references to male behavior saying, "We all married the same man anyway." They have learned that abusive men behave the same way and one woman's story is going to be very similar to another's. They know it is not about the men. After you have told your story one time to a person or people you trust, don't retell it. It's not about him. Yes, his behavior is awful. Yes, he said he loved you. Yes, he lies. Yes, he is untrustworthy. Yes, he has betrayed you and your children. Yes, it is unfair. Yes, it hurts. Yes, Yes, Yes. And *no* he won't change. Why should he? He gets to behave any way he wants and knows you will put up with it. There's no payoff for him in changing. A person who loves you doesn't hurt you, not intentionally, and any physical abuse is intentional. Now are you convinced? No more discussion of him. It's not about the men!

4

Why You Think You Stay

The most confusing thing about domestic violence is trying to figure out why you can't leave your abuser, repeatedly return to him, or get out of one abusive relationship and into another. You've probably had people tell you, or you've told yourself, "I guess I'm co-dependent" or "my dad beat my mom and I said I'd never let that happen to me, but here I am." Or "he has an anger problem and I should help him." Or "he's an alcoholic (or drug addict), and it's a disease, right? I took a vow 'in sickness and health.' I can't leave him if he's sick." Or "my kids need a dad." Or "I don't have a job. He has the money." Or "I keep hoping he'll change. He says he's sorry and things get better sometimes." Or "he's really trying to change." Or "I don't know. I'm just stupid." Or "I'm a magnet. I attract all the wrong men." However, at the time these are exactly the right men. That's why *you* attract and choose *them*.

I'm sure you have read or heard, or perhaps said it yourself, "If I leave he'll kill me." Surprisingly, in my experience, the least common reason women give for staying with their abusers is that they are afraid of being hurt or killed if they leave. I have certainly known women who report this, and they mean it. However, when questioned about resources to escape, they are quite able to identify a means of leaving, yet they continue to assert that it is impossible. Returning to my discussion in chapter 3, this is not an example of "learned helplessness." These women know what they need to do, they know how to leave, but they are not ready to accept the reality of their situation—that nothing they can do will change their abuser's behavior. They certainly do not perceive themselves as helpless in their ability to effect change in their abuser. In fact, they persist in "helping" too much. They just haven't applied the "help" to themselves. They keep trying to find a solution to the problem of his violence, and they use fear of death as a way to stay. After all, who can blame them for staying if the consequences for leaving are so dire?

I firmly encourage women to face the reality of death. If a person truly believes her life is in danger, she does not hang around and wait for something awful to happen, especially if she is sitting in a safe place telling others how afraid she is. And if a woman has already left her abuser and is in the safety of the shelter, telling others she didn't leave earlier because she was afraid her abuser would kill her, then what is different now? What became of that fear? If it was possible for her to leave today, she could have left yesterday, last week, or last year.

If you truly fear for your own, or your children's, safety, do whatever it takes to get to safety. Today most states have laws that make stalking and domestic violence a crime. You have legal protection. If you live in a community where help is limited, go to the police, call an attorney, call anyone you can think of who might have some information about services. Treat your abuser as if he were a stranger and threatened you. You would certainly not tolerate such behavior and would take action. Use the same attitude to protect yourself from your abuser.

As I stated earlier, I've seen few women who say physical fear is the reason for not leaving their abusers. When I hear this and explore it further, I usually find illogical thought processes occurring. If you truly fear for your life, the logical thing to do is leave. And if your next thought is *but he won't let me*, then you are going to have to explain how it is he never leaves the house. In extremely rare occasions there are men who actually lock their wives in basements or bedrooms, and these women are truly captives, but in most cases domestic violence happens in very average homes where people have work and school schedules, go shopping, and lead outwardly ordinary lives. Usually there are daily opportunities to grab what you can and get out. If you don't have access to a car, call the police, a friend, relative, the neighbor, and don't think about the baby pictures, the dog, the cat, your favorite book, the new flat screen television, your wedding dress, or any other piece of your life that might slow you down. Nothing is worth more than your life. Pick the kids up at school and head for safety. If you believe that he will kill you, you absolutely cannot stay with him! What you are saying is that as long as you stay you will allow yourself to be tortured and brutalized, and it is only when you leave that you will be killed. If your partner is capable of killing you, he can kill you under any circumstance. You are not safer at home. Plenty of women are "accidentally" injured or killed. Also, if you are in an abusive situation, you may have considered killing yourself. Staying may make life more tenuous than leaving. Do not give up your life for anyone.

My experience has been that when women are confronted with their behavior of staying with a potential murderer, they will define him as *more* dangerous than any other abuser. After all, since living, sleeping, and having sex with a potential killer isn't logical, there has to be a really good reason to stay—this particular abuser, this thug, this madman has to be the biggest and baddest of them all, otherwise why else would she stay? She has to convince herself that there is no police officer, no judge, no jail, no prison, and no army big enough to stop him from harming her. She *has* to stay with him.

I am not discounting the real danger of domestic terrorism. Admittedly there have been cases where victims were physically held prisoner in their homes. These are extreme cases, and we hear about them because the women were indeed able to escape when the opportunities presented themselves. What I am trying to emphasize is that when your life is threatened, and you believe that the person you are with will take your life, there is only one reasonable action—do whatever it takes to get out. It is insane to convince yourself that staying is better than leaving. You are fooling yourself. You and I know that you are afraid to leave, not because he will kill you, but because you are afraid of being lonely and that in your mind is worse than death. Consider what I have just discussed—living every day with the possibility of being injured or killed by the person you love, or killing yourself, is a better choice than saving your life. This shows you that the real reason you stay is far scarier and threatening than actual death.

What if He Says He Will Kill Himself?

Another reason women give for not leaving is that their abusers threaten to kill themselves if they leave. In fact, some men have killed themselves, but more often they killed their wives or girlfriends first and then took their own lives. If you are staying with an abusive man because you believe he will kill himself if you leave, you are saying his life is more valuable than yours. You are saying that you are willing to take responsibility for his actions. If a man is capable of killing himself, he is capable of killing, period. That means he can kill you, your children, and himself. Yes, if he kills himself, you will feel bad, but you will be alive. If you want to stop being abused and stop being a victim, you must stop acting as if your life is worth less than the life of a potential murderer. If you have already left your abuser, and he informs you that he plans to kill himself, you should call the police and have them make a house call to check on his well-being. The proper professionals are the people who should deal with suicide threats, not you. If your abuser is serious about taking his life and he is honest with the authorities, he will be taken into protective custody or to a mental health facility. Trust me, he isn't going to like it there, but if he is serious about suicide, that is where he needs to be. If your abuser says he's going to kill himself, call the police every time without hesitation.

You Are Not "Just Stupid"

Now let's explore some of the other explanations you might have for staying with your abuser. If you are thinking *I guess I'm just stupid*, I can tell you have been in your situation a long time and tried everything you know to make sense of it, but nothing has changed except your age. What you are saying is that you are incapable of discovering the secret to changing your abuser, and since "stupid" must be innate, who could hold you responsible for your own well-being? Maybe you have resigned your situation to the fact that you must be stupid, or maybe you've even said these words out loud. You may feel unable to affect change in the relationship, but I'll bet this thinking doesn't apply to other areas of your life. Do you work outside your home? If so, it follows that someone thinks you have the capacity to perform the work that they are willing to pay you to do. You have marketable skills, and your past and present employers recognize that. If you were indeed stupid, you wouldn't be employed. Now, that doesn't mean one has to be employed to prove intellect. Perhaps you are a homemaker. If you think *I'm just a housewife*, ask yourself what that means. What do you do all day? You probably have a long list of things you do that reveals someone who is well able to organize her day around other family members' schedules. If you are a stay-at-home mom, you are responsible for teaching and caring for your children. That is one of the most important jobs and to do it properly takes a good deal of smarts. If you are employed, you are also managing your time around work and home needs. What skills do you need in order to compete at work and organize and maintain your home? All work, whether paid or unpaid, requires knowledge, time management, personal interaction, flexibility, problem-solving, and the ability to perform each individual aspect of the job, whether you're sweeping a floor or directing a board meeting. All work requires some skill. Your work clearly indicates that you are intellectually capable of making decisions, both small and large. How are you able to perform tasks and use your now acknowledged abilities to do good work, yet be unable to make your relationship better? What allows you to remain in a dangerous situation?

Remember that quote, "Stupid is as stupid does?" If you have enough awareness to know that your situation is detrimental and dangerous, you are not stupid. If you know the appropriate thing to do is to leave, you are not stupid. But yes, you will be behaving stupidly if you stay.

Remember, you didn't enter the relationship believing that you would be unable to manage and control your life; after all, *you chose* this individual for a mate. It was a decision, a choice. Obviously it wasn't a good choice, but *you* were an active partner in the decision. And you didn't make the choice because you were stupid. Instead, you made it from your heart, placing your hope in love. Your intentions were good. You are not responsible for how he behaves, but you are responsible for staying and allowing the abuse to continue. Now you know it is up to you and you cannot use the "stupid" excuse for making the wrong and dangerous choice. It is not stupid to be afraid.

But What about Mom?

Another explanation some women give for staying in abusive relationships is that their mothers were also in abusive relationships. This type of reasoning has been studied and is called "learned behavior." Albert Bandura (1995) is well known for his work in this area and he asserts "modeling" is a way in which we learn from others how to behave in social situations. His theory posits that our thinking is also influenced through observing and imitating others. As children we observe adults behaving in particular ways, and we learn to imitate their actions. Again, Ola Barnett, Cindy Miller-Perrin, and Robin Perrin do an excellent job of presenting pros and cons of this theory as it relates to domestic violence, and again I agree with the cons. According to this theory, if a girl observed her mother being mistreated, she would model the behavior of her mother and also become submissive and allow men to abuse her. Barnett, Miller-Perrin, and Perrin refer to studies by Sharon Mihalic and Delbert Elliott, Center for the Study and Prevention of Violence (1997) and state, "Counting against this theory is the fact that many, if not most, individuals exposed to violent family models do not go on to emulate abusive behaviors later in life" (2005, 35).

When you were a child and wanted to do something that might have been harmful to you, your mother probably said no. Then you probably replied with something like, "But Susie's allowed to do it!" You believed you should be allowed to do whatever Susie was allowed to do. However, your mother, like most of our parents, likely responded with the familiar line, "If Susie jumped off a bridge and killed herself, does that mean you should do it too?" Concerned parents don't want, or knowingly allow, their children to engage in potentially harmful behavior, regardless of who else is doing it. That question about jumping off the bridge was how they taught us *not* to imitate dangerous behavior. We learn not to walk in front of moving cars, not to play on railroad tracks, not to jump into unfamiliar water, not to eat spoiled food, not to pet strange dogs, not to run with scissors, and not to do all those really harmful things that threaten our health and safety. Does it make sense that if you saw your mother engaging in behavior that was emotionally equivalent to walking in front of a moving train that you would choose to do the same?

I have heard many women say that while they were growing up they vowed to themselves they would never marry a man like their abusive fathers or stepfathers, yet there they were, entirely confused, repeating the worn out phrase, "My mother was in an abusive relationship…." Believe me, this is not and never will be the real reason you ended up with your abuser. It does involve your mother, but not in this simplistic, imitative way.

Personally, I find it insulting to all women when someone says that women are in abusive relationships because they saw their mothers being abused. Thinking adults know abuse is wrong, illegal, and painful. Women don't stay in abusive relationships because they think it is acceptable behavior even if they have witnessed it while growing up.

The Anger Problem Excuse

One of my favorite discussions is the "anger problem" excuse used to justify male violence. "My husband/boyfriend has an anger problem. That's why he's violent." If this is the reason you give yourself and others to make sense of his behavior and justify your decision to stay with him, I need to ask, does your partner lose his temper in the grocery store and hit the check-out clerk? How about the bank teller? Ever beat up the paperboy? Ever whack his boss? Now, if the answer to any of these is yes, then I'll agree there's a good possibility your man has an intermittent explosive disorder with a little antisocial personality disorder thrown in. Or if he is a drug user, maybe he's coming down from the methamphetamine and out of control. But he's also probably headed for jail, if not prison, because his outbursts and behavior will lead to arrest and prosecution. (Or, he's on meds and under control.)

Actually, I've never had an affirmative response to those questions. You may not have asked yourself these questions and might be surprised that you never considered that your partner's behavior was different outside the home. Does your house have a magical door that changes your husband when he walks through it? At this point, are you beginning to understand? Your partner *chooses* to behave violently at home because he knows he can get away with it.

The Addiction Excuse

Same thing for the alcohol and/or drug addicted man. Your partner is aware he becomes violent toward you (and possibly your children) when he drinks or uses drugs, and he knows no one is forcing him to indulge in them. Is he getting professional help? If not, that indicates he *chooses* to continue drinking or using drugs as an excuse for acting violently. In addition to being a marriage and family therapist, I am also a substance abuse counselor, and I see plenty of people with addictions who don't beat up their loved ones or other people. In fact, some people become mellow and affable or feel good when they use drugs or alcohol. Glenda Kantor and Murray Straus of the Family Research Laboratory, University of New Hampshire (in Zubretsky and Digirolamo 1987), report that 76 percent of abusive incidents happen when there is *no* alcohol use involved. The belief that addiction causes men to behave violently toward their partners and that treating the addiction will end the violence can be decidedly harmful to battered women because it gets men off the hook. "The alcohol provides a ready and socially acceptable excuse for their violence … Battered women with drug-dependent partners … consistently report that during recovery the abuse not only continues, but often escalates creating greater levels of danger than existed prior to their partners' abstinence" (1987). Alcohol is not the cause of your partner's violence. Now you can stop using that as a reason to stand by him.

The Bipolar Excuse

The same holds true for what has become the ubiquitous "bipolar" excuse. For many years I worked for a regional mental health hospital, and I know scores of people who have bipolar disorder. This disorder causes sufferers to have difficulty managing their mood. Sometimes a bipolar person will be very depressed, and other times they'll be manic, or very "up." Certainly, during a manic episode, a bipolar person's behavior may become unpredictable and not make a lot of sense to others. But violence is not a condition or symptom of bipolar disorder. There are appropriate medications to address the symptoms of bipolar disorder, and they are generally effective for most people. As with most medications, there may be unwanted side effects. If your partner has been professionally diagnosed with bipolar disorder, declines to take the medication because of side effects, and is violent, again he is *choosing* to use his illness as an excuse to hurt you. You are not obligated to remain with a violent person who refuses to get medical or psychiatric help. His life is not more valuable than yours. The loss of your life will not cure him.

What If I'm Co-dependent?

Perhaps you have labeled yourself "co-dependent" and used this as the reason why you stay with an abuser. I keep hearing co-dependency as a reason for staying with a violent person, but I don't know what it means in the context of an abusive relationship. I keep asking for an explanation, but I still haven't gotten one. Certainly, humans need one another. We are interdependent. Does being co-dependent mean if you or your partner leaves or dies the other can't continue to live? Logically, of course, the answer is "no," but you may feel that you will die if you are not connected to your abuser. Here is where we get closer to the real reason for staying, but it isn't your abuser you need connection with. The use of the word *co-dependent* has become jargon. Defining yourself as co-dependent gives you a way to explain your behavior even if you have no idea what it means. Some reason is better than no reason.

When a woman is dependent on her abuser for income, it is more difficult, but not impossible, to leave. I have actually heard women say they stay with their abusers because they are afraid their children will starve if they leave. They actually use the word "starve." If you have found yourself thinking your children will starve, it is time for some rational thinking. Are people in this country starving? Do you walk down the streets in your city or neighborhood and literally see children with swollen stomachs and emaciated bodies? No. There may be some degree of hunger, but there are also community food pantries, food stamps, soup kitchens, and other places for people to obtain help. This country has an abundance of food. People are not starving. You and your children will not starve if you leave your abuser. Yes, you may have to struggle financially. You may have to live in a shelter. You may have to find employment or apply for social services. You may not be able to keep the material aspects of your life, but more importantly, you and your children will *have* a life. My intent in this discussion is not to minimize problems faced by women with few resources, but to take a realistic look at available options. Other women have faced similar situations and they took advantage of community resources and programs that assist with housing, food, medical care, clothing, and legal issues. You are not alone. Instead of seeing limitations to freedom and responsibility, you can learn self-reliance and depend on your own strength and knowledge.

Marta, a member of one of my women's groups, is an example of someone who's had to face dire financial consequences. Marta was in the United States illegally from Central America. She barely spoke English and my Spanish is only passable, so I recruited a translator to help with individual sessions. (Whether this work takes place in group or a one-on-one session, the work is done in sequence and has positive results.) Marta was the oldest of five children raised in a small town. Her parents were not rich but were able to support their family adequately. Marta liked school and her teachers frequently commented on her intelligence. She particularly enjoyed studying science and dreamed of becoming a biologist, but she was the oldest child and her parents did not encourage her to further her education. They made it clear that they could not afford to send her to college and if anyone went, it would be the youngest brother, who did especially well in his studies. There were not many opportunities for work, and Marta had little hope for an independent future. When she met Oscar, he already had one "wife," but they had not been married by the church, so Marta did not consider him truly married. Marta had heard rumors that Oscar hit his other woman, but she dismissed these as exaggerations. After all, the other wife was said to love to spend money and could not be trusted. Oscar seemed ambitious and promised her that he would take her to the United States if she married him. Marta began to dream of opportunities that she wouldn't find in her small town. She agreed to marry. Oscar left the other wife and he and Marta married in the church—a real marriage. Within the first two years of marriage, Oscar began acting jealously, accusing Marta of wanting to be with other men, following her to the market, and calling her names. When she became pregnant, he started hitting her and telling her the baby was not his. Marta didn't know what to do. Her parents wondered what was wrong when they saw their daughter look so sad when she should have been looking forward to a new baby. When Marta and Oscar told them about their plans to move to the United States, they hoped everything would be good for Marta, but they knew they would miss seeing their first grandchild. Oscar had spent months making plans to cross the border and when the day came, he and Marta crossed and made their way to a safe home. Several months later their daughter was born, and Marta's life became centered on caring for her new baby. Oscar continued to be controlling and jealous and the abuse became worse. Marta was stuck in a bad marriage in an unfamiliar country whose language she did not know. On the surface it seems she was truly unable to leave him because she had no way to care for herself and her daughter. However, when Marta lived in Central America, she was near her family, who would have helped her leave him. Why hadn't she leave him then when there was family near and she was familiar with resources?

Eventually Marta became a virtual prisoner in her home. Oscar had a few friends and occasionally invited a co-worker and his wife to dinner. One evening, Oscar and his friend went to the store to buy some forgotten items for dinner. While they were gone, Marta confided in the friend's wife and told her about the abuse and her fear of Oscar. The woman was a godsend and told Marta she didn't have to stay, there were places where she could go for help and she could take her child, too. They made plans for the next week when Oscar would be at work. The woman drove Marta and her daughter to a local shelter, where she was given a warm welcome, and Marta took her first steps toward freedom.

When we investigated her reasons for staying with Oscar, some were obvious—no work visa, the threat of deportation, her inability to communicate, and her fear of losing custody of her small child. The shelter staff helped Marta apply to immigration for a work visa, which she received. While waiting to obtain the legal documents, Marta and I got to work and Marta learned the reasons why she stayed so long with Oscar. When she completed counseling, Marta had a job and income sufficient for her and her daughter. She was learning English easily as she began interacting with her co-workers, and she acquired housing she could afford. Most importantly, she avoided becoming involved with another man, her co-worker, who also appeared controlling. Marta was flattered by his attention, and she was tempted to give in to his requests to move in with him. He could have easily provided for Marta and her daughter very well. Fortunately, Marta was able to identify all the warning signs of an abuser, and she was now fully aware of her own emotional vulnerability. Even though she would continue to struggle to pay the bills, she chose to go it alone.

Marta is just one example of a woman who faced legitimate financial hardship yet was able to find freedom, but only after she achieved emotional freedom. When it seems impossible, ask yourself what you would do if there was no man in your life and you were in the same financial situation. Chances are you would find help, get a job, acquire housing, use food stamps, move if you had to, and all the while you would be showing your children how to overcome life's challenges. With each success you build more self-efficacy and self-esteem. Women who have not been abused accomplish these things all the time. Or they choose healthy partners to help out. Abused women are no less capable or smart. You *can* change your life, and if you want to live, *you will have to change* regardless of the challenges you face.

My Kids Need A Father

Another common reason women stay with an abuser is they believe their kids need a dad. My response to that is, "What for?" We've already discussed the financial reasons and determined that, even though it might be difficult, you can make it. Why do your children need an abusive man in the house? To teach your little boy how to be an abuser too? To teach your little girl to be afraid of men? To show your kids who's in charge? To teach them to sleep lightly? To teach them that home is not a safe place? To teach them how to keep shameful family secrets? To teach them how long it takes for broken bones to heal? To teach them how to get blood out of the carpet? To teach them how their mother will eat without her front teeth? To teach them how loudly one has to scream before the neighbors call the police? I realize those last questions create some ugly mental pictures. However, this *is* the reality of domestic violence. This *is* the reality that your children see and learn when they live with an abusive father.

I am always amazed at how often I hear a woman talk at length about how abusive her husband or boyfriend is, followed by the remark that she won't leave, "Because he's a good father." Read this carefully and pay attention. *A man cannot be a good father if he hurts a child's mother.* When a mother is hurt and in pain, her child will also suffer. Pain, whether physical or emotional, keeps a mother from being fully able to attend to her child's needs. If you are always focused on your abuser, you will have little energy and time to give your children the love and attention they need. Many would say that once you become a mother, that is your most important job. A *good* father does not interfere with or impede a mother's ability to do the job of mothering.

I do agree that children should have fathers. It seems to be the natural order for human beings. Families have historically and universally tended to look somewhat alike, with mothers, fathers, and children living in various household arrangements. There is a difference, however, between biologically fathering a child and being in a father role. When women say that children should have a father, what they mean is they believe that children should have a man in the father role. A man with all the attendant behavior that goes along with that role—caring, teaching, protecting, providing. But there are many times when there is no man in that role in a household. Fathers die in accidents or are killed in wars. What about the woman who chooses to be artificially inseminated because her window of fertility is closing and she has not found a partner? Over the years, and with a lot of scientific innovations, men no longer have to actively participate in the fathering process with the prospective mother. For example, artificial insemination has allowed many women to become mothers and the sperm donors aren't even aware of the fact they have fathered children. Artificial insemination also allows lesbian couples to rear children together without a "father." Not everyone gets a father, but children in these families, either single parent or "two mommies," can still enjoy emotionally healthy lives.

Have you used the "children should have a father" excuse as a reason to stay with your abuser? Do you know, or do you know about, people who grew up without fathers and who turned out happy and healthy? Certainly, you know that it is possible, and not uncommon. Often, when I explore this line of thinking with women, we come to the real reason they believe their children need fathers. "I never had a father who was there for me, so I want my kids to have a father." Ah, it's really about *you* then, isn't it? It is true in my own life and I find it in other parents—we give our children what *we* needed as children. Whatever we thought was very important but was missing for us, we want to make sure our children have. If we were embarrassed by our poor clothing, we buy our kids the latest styles. If we didn't get to play sports, we sign them up for every community sports team. If we felt left out because we couldn't go to the prom, we live for our children's every high school dance. And if you missed your father terribly, whether you knew him or not, you will not want your children to experience that same feeling of pain. You will want to give your children what was important to you. However, when you spend your time and effort giving your children what *you* want, you are not paying attention to what *they* actually need and want. And life comes full circle, with each generation giving something that is meaningless to their children. Please do not use your child as a reason to stay with an abusive man. You are mistaken if you confuse your children's needs with your own.

Earlier I said I believe children should have fathers. More importantly, however, is that fathers should behave in a healthy manner and fulfill the role expectations I mentioned earlier—caring, teaching, protecting, and providing. Abusive fathers are not healthy role models. When, for whatever reason, fathers were not wanted in a relationship, or were not available, women have always carried on solo. Your children should not have to live with an abusive man in order to fulfill *your* wish.

But I Promised

Your moral beliefs might be another reason you give for staying in the relationship. Like Janet, who had many years invested in her relationship, you may think you have to do all you can, go the last mile, before you can leave. In your heart you know that for your own future peace of mind, you must do whatever it takes before you give up on your family and the person you love. You believe it's the moral thing to do. You promised "'til death do you part." You might have religious beliefs that reinforce the idea that divorce is wrong. Additionally, if your current marriage or relationship is the second or third, you, like many others, may believe that if you end this one you will be a "three-time loser." One more divorce will prove you are a failure. I frequently hear women state their fear of failing one more time. I ask them to define failure and usually the response is related to time. We have been taught that the longer one is married, the more successful the marriage. We celebrate the length of time couples have been together in newspaper articles—couple celebrates fifty year anniversary! How often have you seen a photo of a young couple with the title, "Couple celebrates divorce after six successful years of marriage?" That sounds unusual, but there is more than one way to measure success. Perhaps it's time to redefine success based on how the relationship served its purpose. For instance, if the original reason for the marriage was to increase income, have 2.5 children, and provide health insurance, then it was successful if these goals were met. If the purpose of the marriage was to prevent two people from being lonely and bored, then it is successful as long as it serves that function. Redefining success and failure in a relationship may help you realize the purpose of your marriage and give you the freedom to take an honest look at yourself and your relationships. The length of time you've been together is not the measure of success. A successful marriage is measured by how the needs of each family member are met. It is impossible for everyone's needs—emotional, physical, spiritual, financial, and social—to be met 100 percent of the time. However, a functional family will try to meet each person's needs as much as possible because they genuinely care about each other. It is entirely possible to have had several short successful marriages if the needs of the people involved were met. If your needs change and are no longer being met, to continue the relationship would make it "unsuccessful." When you are being physically threatened and hurt, your need for safety and security is not being met—your relationship, no matter how many years it has endured, is not successful. If you feel you have to give it your all before you can leave your abuser, I wish you well and hope you are able to leave with your life and the least amount of physical harm. You will not escape without emotional and psychological injury, and the injuries will increase the longer you stay.

When your sense of self is deeply enmeshed with another person, it feels impossible to detach from him. You may believe you can't leave your abuser because he's your soul mate—the only person in the world destined by heaven to be the perfect match for you. After all, it's magical, meant to be. This must be true because it *feels* different from any other relationship. Usually, when I hear the word *soul mate,* I start screaming. Not really, but I certainly feel like it. I've never received an adequate answer when I ask what a soul mate is, but I do get plenty of women who believe they are not complete without their partners. What if my soul mate is in China? Am I destined to be half soulless if I never have the money to go there? And even if I went there, it's a big country. I may never find him, and even if I do, what if he's already married or he's only twelve years old? I guess I'd be destined to have only half a soul! With all the marriages, divorces, and remarriages going on, who could keep track of where the other half of one's soul might end up? Or do we start halving the halves until pieces of our souls are all just scattered about? The idea of a soul mate is beginning to sound a little ridiculous, isn't it?

Let's think rationally about this phenomenon. Each of us is capable of loving many different people. You probably know plenty of people who have been married more than once or had more than one loving relationship. If you ask them, they will say they loved each of the people they were involved with at the time. Each love was different, but it was real and the relationship was meaningful. There are many healthy, non-abusive people in the world who you are capable of loving and with whom you are compatible. An abuser is not your heaven-sent soul mate unless you chose, in this lifetime, to live in hell.

Hope

Hope is another common reason why women stay in abusive relationships. So many women tell me, "I keep hoping he'll change." Hope will keep you going for a long time. Any change, no matter how insignificant, can be a sign that he's changing. When Janet decided she had to leave Darren because she believed he would kill her, either purposefully or accidentally, she saved more than a thousand dollars in a secret account. It was difficult. Darren had used up all their credit on a bucketful of credit cards and Janet, who paid the bills, was scrambling to cover monthly costs. She had half the money she thought she needed to escape, but she hadn't begun making concrete plans. Some hope remained. After several months without physical abuse, she became desperate to pay Darren's debts. Her savings would pay only a small fraction of the debt, but she had convinced herself that Darren had

The Saber-Toothed Tiger

changed, even though the threats and belittling behavior continued. She reasoned that maybe if they no longer had the financial stress, he would change even more. She used all her savings and made a payment on an account. Stupid? Probably. Hopeful? Yes. Darren's behavior did not change. Why should it? It certainly wasn't to his advantage to change. He wasn't engaged in therapy or discussing how he needed to change. He had everything he wanted or could intimidate Janet into giving him what he wanted. After the next incident of abuse when she was choked to the point of nearly passing out, Janet began saving again. Hope was dying.

Women hope. They hope their partners will go back to being the charming men they married. Then they could get on with living happily ever after. Wasn't he a nice guy once upon a time? Women hope men will stop drinking or drugging because they think then the terror will stop. Women hope the last arrest and jail time will be a wake-up call. Women hope if men's parents know, the men will be ashamed and stop hitting. Women hope if they lose five pounds, they will be loveable again. Women hope more money will make men happy. Women hope there will be a cure for men's "anger problem." Women hope they can forget and forgive. Women hope Jesus, Buddha, God, or Allah will hear their prayers and promises and intervene. Women hope for a miracle. Yes, hope will take you a long way. Hope will keep you living in hell and take you to your grave.

Hope is worthwhile only if it is realistic. Look for hard evidence to support your hope. I said "evidence," not words. If you have been in an abusive relationship for any length of time, you've already heard all the lying words you ever need to hear. Words are not evidence. <u>They are only words, without intent, meant to manipulate you into staying around.</u> A significant change in behavior is evidence. Has your partner independently engaged in counseling? In other words, did he, on his own and without your prompting and reminding, find a counselor, call for an appointment, and attend? People who are genuinely concerned about their bad behavior find help in order to change because it disturbs them to hurt other people, particularly those they love. If your abuser has not done something to significantly change his behavior, your hope is groundless. What are you hoping *for*?

Many women think they stay in a marriage or relationship for the best of reasons—to maintain their families. Certainly this is admirable and well-intentioned, however distorted. Family as a haven of love, caring, and support for each member is not "maintained" when there is violence against any of its members. What is being "maintained" is a group of people living in the same house where there is pain and fear—an emotionally desolate landscape. Again, women hope their partners will go back to being the charming men they married. (If indeed they were ever charming. I know women who married men who were physically abusive to them even before the wedding, and they went right ahead and said "I do" anyway.) Are you waiting for your partner to return to being how he was in the past? Did he seem like a decent guy once upon a time? Are you waiting until you can get on with the dream of having a happy, healthy family? Ask yourself the next obvious question. What if he will never be the man you thought he was or wanted him to be? What are you waiting *for*?

5

Sex: The Last Excuse to Stay

What would we do without sex? Everyone knows what sex is for, right? Sure, procreation. At least that's the way it is in the animal kingdom. Two squirrels get together, they don't even have to actually know one another well, they just have sex and the world welcomes a bunch of little squirrels. Well, maybe not welcomes, but you get the idea. Animals are blessed with wonderful, if not sometimes odd, physical characteristics meant to attract the opposite sex. Male peacocks have elaborately colored tail feathers that they display as they strut around, inviting the females to admire their beauty. The males of the big-horned sheep family use strength and stamina to attract the opposite sex. They charge one another, banging their oversized horns against their opponent's in the hopes that a female will find that attractive. Regardless of the varied ways nature has found to aid in the procreation of different species, the results are the same—more of the same types of critters.

Then there are humans. What other creature in the world exhibits such ongoing creativity? Before we discuss sexual creativity, let me digress a bit about simple, or not so simple, human creativity in general. First, let's consider skiing. Humans find a huge snow-covered mountain and some flimsy sticks and instead of asking, "How the hell am I going to stay safe on this mountain?" they exclaim, "I've got an idea! Let's strap these little sticks onto our feet and risk our lives by hurling our bodies down the side of this mountain at neck-breaking speed! Better yet, let's leap off an incredibly dangerous cliff and try doing some jumps and twists while we're barreling down the slope!" Creativity. Another example is technology. Humans have developed incomprehensible communication systems, television, computers, and wireless telephones. One would think these wonderful inventions would create a plethora of opportunities for education, intelligent exchange of ideas, and meaningful communication between governments that might lead to peace and prosperity. But how do most humans use these wonderful inventions? They engage in mindless chatter, purchase products they don't really want because they want to be the one who wins with the lowest bid, watch mind-numbing comedies and pornography, put up with ubiquitous "spam," and communicate through misspelled, abbreviated text messages of questionable importance. These are just two examples of how, in our moments of boredom, we humans can create novelty and enjoyment out of almost any device or situation. I would say human beings are overachieving in their creativity. Unfortunately, humans can also be dangerously creative, which enhances the thrill and gives an edge of excitement to any endeavor. And that's where we return to the topic of sex and our dangerous creativity.

It is not difficult to conceptualize how humans can be sexually creative. Indeed, humans may be at their most creative when it involves sex. No boring quickies-in-the-spring babies-in-the-fall routine for us! (Okay, maybe for some of us.) No, we're human beings! Homo sapiens! People—top of the food chain! We can't do ordinary sex! We have to be creative! Just like the mountain and the sticks, the cell phone and the Internet, we have to find other uses, besides procreation, for sex. We even construct rules and regulations around sex. For example, states have laws regarding the appropriate age for consensual sex, and historically some states have made laws that dictate who can marry and have sex with whom, where, and how it can be done. Not only do we have a legal code regarding sex, we have religious teachings about sex. Do it certain ways and you will burn in hell forever. (And still people push that envelope.) We add layers of cultural behaviors and dress and attach sexual meaning to them. We make movies and videos that enable us to enjoy sexual feelings vicariously. We've outdone ourselves in the sexual inventiveness area. We use sex for every occasion. In the United States we can't even sell toothpaste without the help of a sexual image. Sex has become our all-time, all-purpose product!! However, I must caution you, creativity can be dangerous, especially when it comes to sex.

By now you might be wondering how this topic relates to you as an abused woman. In the last chapter, I explored some of the reasons women give for staying in abusive relationships. At some point in the counseling sessions, when we've found these reasons wanting, someone laughs nervously and says, "But the sex is *so* good!" Others nod and laugh with understanding. They expect the conversation to end. What's left to say? Great sex explains it all! How could anyone leave good sex? After all, this one man, this abuser, is magical. Sex with him could never be replaced. Consider how convenient this thinking is for him. An abusive man will encourage this belief. It's another avenue for control.

Like many women, you may feel awkward and shy when discussing sex. All too often, women have experienced rape, incest, and/or childhood sexual abuse and the pain of the past prevents women from enjoying sex. Sometimes, women have physical or medical issues that interfere with their desire for and enjoyment of intercourse. However, this discussion is necessary and can provide insight into how you may be using sex in order to keep your relationship with your abuser. Do you think sex with your partner is exceptional and that if you leave him, you will not experience sex in the same way ever again? What makes sex with this person exceptional? Have you experienced good sex with anyone else? Women who have had more than one sexual partner and who enjoy sex usually admit they have had satisfying sex with other people. Perhaps you have experienced the same thing. I propose what to some may be a radical thought. *The best sex you have should be with yourself.* Think about it. No one knows your body like you do, or at least no one should. You are responsible for your body's health and you need to know how your body works. You should know, through education or experience, how your body responds to medications, allergens, food, alcohol, fear, anger, happiness, sex, and sad movies. Women need to take individual responsibility for their own sexual pleasure instead of expecting it from men. Certainly, it's helpful if the guy is fairly adept and also knows his body well, but they all are pretty much similarly equipped!

Here's where women get creative with sex and use it for another purpose. "I'll make my pleasure his responsibility, so if I'm not satisfied he'll feel inadequate and try to make it up to me in other ways." We all know how many ways we can invent to have things made up to us—romance, diamonds, marriage, house, car, clothes, sweet talk, another baby, promises, affection, and the all time biggie, eternal love and devotion. Goodness, think what could occur if women were responsible for their own orgasms!

What better way to permanently bind another human being to us, first sexually and eventually biologically, than by having children? Even healthy women can behave this way, but for women in abusive relationships, sex takes on a more necessary meaning. Women in abusive relationships have a need for visibility. Notice I said *need*, not *want*. That is important. I explore this idea further in chapters eleven and twelve, so please accept this as fact for the time being. If you are with a man who is abusive, you understand. You use sex as a tool. You hope sex with your partner will make you visible to him. You might think *if only I can get emotionally close enough to him, if I can break through to that real loving inner person I think he is, he'll have to realize he loves me. He will know* how much I love him and he'll have to know how he's hurt me. Then he will really love me and all of this violence will end and we'll be happy. When you think like this, you are being creative with sex because you're using it to validate the fact that you are loveable, desirable, and acceptable. Sex is often a necessary tool for abused women because it directly relates to connection with a particular type of person, and that person has all the characteristics of an abuser. If sex, which is usually considered the closest, most intimate act, can no longer make you visible, then your hope dies.

A very sad thing happens when women realize sex isn't working the way they need it to work. There comes a time when the truth can no longer be denied. If you have experienced this you know exactly how it feels. It happens when you are having sex with your partner and you want him to truly *see you* and you are hoping this wonderful sexual feeling will make you visible to him. You can't help but think sex has to feel the same way for him as it does to you. But when sex is finished, maybe just seconds after orgasm, you know your desire to be visible, to connect with your partner did not happen—you are still invisible. There is a fleeting moment, maybe less that a second (before you push it far away), when you experience a foreboding sensation, a feeling of total emptiness, darkness, a void, absolute emotional isolation. It is in that brief time that you know you are entirely alone and it is the saddest feeling, like death. I think it takes a long time for a woman to acknowledge the reality of that feeling and what it means for her. That feeling is the place where she admits she is not loved or visible. She knows at that moment that no amount of love or sex can change her abuser. Sex is usually used as the last excuse to stay, and once sex is recognized as manipulation and validation, it signals the end of hope.

After leaving your abuser, and despite knowing how you might have been using sex in your relationship, it would not be unusual to deliberately go out and engage in sex with someone in order to prove that you don't use sex to validate that you are "lovable." Perhaps you think you will engage in sex purely for pleasure. When women in my group have tried this, they inevitably report that they couldn't deny the reality of their purpose. It was not sex they wanted, it was validation. They wanted confirmation that they are desirable. They wanted the sweet words. They wanted the attention. In other words, they wanted to be seen, to be visible. Good-naturedly, the women blame me for ruining their sex lives. However, should you decide to experiment, you will likely find that you don't need a particular man, an "exceptional" man, or any man at all to have good sex. With that, the last excuse to stay with an abuser goes out the window.

Of course, sex as manipulation and validation is not confined to abused women or even women in general. Men are just as creative. As I said, it's the all-purpose product. Don't misunderstand; creative sex can be wonderful and exciting when used in a healthy way and when the people involved are in control of the sex, not being controlled by it. Remember, humans give meaning to the sexual act. You should own it, it should never own you. Nothing and no one should ever own you.

Sex can be fun and creative, but also dangerous. Not just because of the oft-repeated risk of sexually transmitted diseases or unwanted pregnancy. Yes, AIDS can kill you, but so can the abusive man you choose to have sex with in an attempt to get him to *really* love you and stop hurting you. Women in abusive relationships are often sexually demeaned and debased. Regrettably, the fear that keeps them enslaved can drive them to demean others, including the children they love so deeply. The following example is painful to relate, but it perfectly illustrates how strong the desire is to use sex as an excuse to remain with an abuser and how desperate a woman can become. In her fear, and mistaken belief that she would be visible to her abuser, a woman I know agreed to have sex with her young teenage daughter while her abuser watched. It was what he required before he would have sex with the woman. The word "desperate" doesn't even begin to describe her behavior. She didn't agree to his demands out of fear of being killed by him. She had a greater fear of living with loneliness, the Saber-Toothed Tiger. How else can this despicable act be explained?

I have repeatedly said that humans are dangerously creative at times. It is when you use sex to fool yourself that it becomes the most dangerous. Sex is dangerous when you choose to believe that good sex is possible with only one person, when you falsely elevate his value. Sex is dangerous when you believe good sex will make you visible. Sex is dangerous when good sex becomes more important than the well-being of children. Sex is dangerous when good sex makes up for the beatings and bruises. Sex is dangerous when good sex is worth more than your freedom or your life. Sex is dangerous when you convince yourself that good sex is the same as good love. Sex is dangerous when you believe that good sex will cover your shame.

6

Preparing to Meet the Saber-Toothed Tiger

I have now explored all the reasons battered women use in order to stay with their abusers, and you have discovered there are healthier ways to get what you need than staying in an abusive relationship. You can find a job, or you can engage in a relationship with a non-abuser who can provide the same material benefits. You can have children with healthy, non-abusive men, or you can raise your children independently or with help from community and family. Humans are interdependent, and you can choose healthy people to have as intimates in your life, which doesn't mean you are innately "co-dependent." Although drug and alcohol use can make it easier to be abusive, people with addictions are not by nature violent and abusive. Don't blame addiction for violence. Hold the abuser responsible for all of his behavior and choices. The same goes for anger. If he is able to control his actions in public, he can do the same at home. Don't accept the inevitability of abuse because your parents practiced it. You are not your parents. Know that sex is not an emotional connection. It doesn't mean you are loved. You will know when hope is gone, but you don't have to wait until the end. Your abuser is not all-powerful. You can escape physical abuse by informing the police, going to a shelter, or telling someone who can help you escape. You can move, and depending on the severity of abuse and fear, you can be given a new identity. All of these options have been presented to the women I've helped, and they were able to make changes that led to freedom and happiness.

Now it's time to explore the one reason you and other women choose abusers, and why you stay with, or may repeatedly engage in, abusive relationships. Your behavior springs from a fear so great that you will endure any abuse to keep it at bay. First understand that the fear does not begin within the abusive relationship. It starts much earlier. Every abused woman who stayed in a relationship, or left one abusive situation for another, understands what I mean when I describe the feelings that arise when they considered leaving. The feeling of fear is so great it feels like death. And for you and other abused women, the feeling is very real.

What do you think will happen if you end the abusive relationship once and for all? Do you get a feeling of panic and fear when you think about forever? If you haven't been in this situation, it might seem unbelievable that leaving an abusive relationship can be scarier than staying. But for the survivor, that is the reality. Usually when a woman first leaves an abusive relationship, she feels exhilarated. She has overcome her fears and indecisiveness and taken that huge step away from her abuser. She is justifiably proud of herself. This act is something she never thought she could accomplish. However, after the first several weeks of separation, most women begin to experience a strong desire to return. They feel anxious and fearful and don't understand why. Logically they know they are in a better, safer place. Like them, you might be thinking *I really must be crazy because I keep thinking of going back.* Rationally you know it is dangerous and you also know if you go back, nothing will change. In fact, it probably will get worse because you will be giving your abuser permission to continue his abusive behavior. At this point you may feel very confused and begin to agree with the negative things your abuser said to you about being crazy, or weak, and that you will never make it without him. You are unaware that fear is driving your behavior and thinking, and you may have a strong longing to return. Let's spend a little time investigating possible futures.

What if You Don't Go Back?

What do you think will happen to him if you *don't* go back? Many women tell me they are concerned that their abusers won't be able to take care of themselves. Are you concerned that your partner is unable to take care of himself, pay the bills, or feed the dog? If this is the case, I have to ask, is he stupid? If you are concerned about his ability to take care of mundane chores or adequately care for himself, then indeed you are sending the message that you believe he is stupid and incompetent. Why would you choose a man who is ineffectual and unable to complete daily tasks? In all likelihood your partner can figure out how to do all of life's everyday tasks.

What do you think is going to happen to *you* if you don't go back? What happens if you get divorced or stay away from your abuser? You will do what you need to do in order to live as independently as you can with the resources and skills you have. You may be confused at this point because your conclusion that your abuser can take care of himself and your acknowledgment that you can create your own independent life are at odds with your desire to go back to him. It isn't logical at all. You know it's better to stay away, you know you can find a way to make a living (if you aren't already), and you know he really doesn't need you to survive.

Now you are nearing the heart of the matter, the dark shadowy form at the back of the cave—the loneliness, the saber-toothed tiger. It is getting scary and the truth is near. The saber-toothed tiger is stalking you and you sense him in the shadows. You have arrived at the crucial place, the dark cave where you can no longer deny the existence of the frightful tiger waiting to pounce. But before you are ready to face the tiger, you have a little work to do. Let's prepare for that meeting.

Preparing to Meet the Saber-Toothed Tiger

Before we go further, I would like you to do the following exercise. Get a sheet of paper and a pencil. Close your eyes and think back to your childhood. Try to remember back as far as possible. Start at your first memory and move forward in time, recalling the days of your childhood. Recall special times such as your first day of school, holidays, summer vacations, birthdays, junior high, high school, school dances, and graduation. Also think about the very ordinary days, and as you reminisce, pay close attention to the events of early childhood until junior high. As you recall particular events and situations, try to reconnect with the feelings you had at the time, especially your feelings about family. If the feelings become uncomfortable, remind yourself that you are no longer back there in your childhood. This is simply an exercise. Try to re-experience the feelings you had while growing up and identify each one. It is perfectly normal if you are only able to identify one or two. Usually, there is a general feeling that pervades our memories. As you return to the days of childhood, focus on the one feeling that seems to stand out for you. Be sure to use words that describe feelings, not behavior. For instance, saying "I felt normal" does not describe a feeling. Use words such as *satisfied, happy, afraid,* or *angry*—words that describe emotions. Perhaps you felt sad as you thought about your childhood. Sometimes it is difficult to return to those feelings, but you are about to uncover the reasons why, and that will help you overcome the past. When you have identified your feelings, write down one to three words that describe how you felt *most of the time* during childhood.

Now that you have identified primary feelings from your early years, next write down three to five things you believed about yourself during your childhood. Write down how you came to believe those things. For example, if you believed you were a good student, you would write that you believed it because you earned As and Bs on your report cards. If, on the other hand, you believed that you were too tall and this was not a good attribute, you might write that you believed this because classmates made negative comments about your height, most people were shorter than you, or no one *ever* asked you to dance. When you are finished, put your lists aside. We will return to them later after we explore childhood a little more.

7

Emotional Oatmeal

Imagine that you are a little girl who every day since the day you are born until the day you leave home is served oatmeal by your parents. Yep, 365 days a year—oatmeal. It doesn't matter if it is a holiday or your birthday or company is over for dinner. You get oatmeal. And it is plain oatmeal, no sugar, no maple syrup, no milk, no raisins, and none of those fruit-flavored individual microwave servings. Nope. Just plain, unadulterated oatmeal. Sometimes it might be a little thicker or thinner depending on the amount of water and cooking time, but every day of your whole life, every meal, every snack, every special occasion—oatmeal. It fills your stomach and keeps you alive but not well nourished. You'd be a lot healthier with some protein and calcium, not to mention all those other vitamins and minerals so essential for good health. But you get by on the oatmeal. You're alive.

Maybe one day your parents take you to visit some relatives or friends and you notice that the children in those families have different foods to eat. They have bread with jelly, carrots, potatoes, rice, chicken, and beef. And they can ask for more and get it! So when you go home you think, *I'll ask for something different.* And you do. You ask in your sweetest voice with your brightest smile and all the hope in the world in your heart. "May I please have something other than oatmeal, please?" Your heart is in your throat. Did they hear? Do they care? Do I matter? Am I visible? Then your mother opens her mouth and says, "You're being silly (or dumb or a pain in the ass), you've always had lots of different kinds of food. What kind of parents do you think we are?" Now that doesn't make sense to you. You think, *Was I wrong? Maybe it's me. Maybe my perception is way off. Is there something wrong with me? I could have sworn I get only oatmeal.* But this is your mother. Would she mislead you? You don't like to think that would be true, so you adapt. Perhaps you have made a big mistake. As a result, at the next meal you expect something different on your plate or in your bowl. Here it comes. What will it be? The bowl sits before you. You open your hope-filled eyes and see—oatmeal. And, along with the same old oatmeal, you get the message, "Don't disturb our reality." You learn you are the "oatmeal" kid and your perception of your life and your reality is considerably different from that of your parents.

You continue growing (albeit slowly and not as tall and healthy as you would if you had a balanced diet), and you continue to meet schoolmates who have a variety of foods in their healthy lunches. You see movies in which people have incredible choices for food and they enjoy it, relish it, and they are happy and well fed. As a teenager you might begin demanding a varied diet, but your parents continue to give you oatmeal and tell you to stop bothering them. Along with the oatmeal you may get messages like, "It costs too much," "You're not smart enough, or thin enough, or pretty enough," or "You don't deserve anything else, and you're ungrateful to boot!" So you eat your oatmeal. Inside you know you should have vegetables, meat, and fruit. *You know.* And as you get older you even experiment a little—sneak out to McDonald's with a friend, order a dish of ice cream, taste some forbidden fruit. But it doesn't quite fill the empty stomach and feed your soul like some good, wholesome, mother-loving, home-cooked food.

Then there comes a day, a magical, unbelievable day. You meet someone, a man, and he offers to give you something wonderful. Something sugary and sweet, warm and creamy—chocolate! Imagine how your taste buds respond. The rush of glucose releases a cascade of feel-good serotonin in your brain. You enjoy an extraordinary sense of well-being, contentment, and joy. Relief! Finally, finally, no oatmeal! Not only is it not oatmeal, it's something beyond vegetables, beyond steak, beyond any food you've ever tasted! Wow! You never want to eat oatmeal again. You really, really want rich sweet wonderful chocolate! And how do you feel about that special, awesome somebody who introduced you to this delicious feeling? You love him! You adore him! You are more than grateful. You might even say you would die for him. After all, he's the one who gave you this feeling, isn't he? This man and the sweetness and the breathtaking feeling are inseparable. He's the only one who can give you this wonderful, exceptional feeling!

What I have just described is the childhood experience of women who are attracted to abusive, controlling men. They grow up with an emotional life equivalent to oatmeal; receiving enough care to keep them alive but not enough love to flourish. After a lifetime of emotional oatmeal, they are attracted to men who know how to give the sweetness and chocolate. These women respond to, and fall in love with, the opposite extreme of oatmeal—the chocolate sugar rush. They are not attracted to the men who offer a healthy balanced diet.

When you are really hungry, you don't take a lot of time or make much effort to find or prepare the absolute best meal. You grab whatever is handy. And when you grow up emotionally starved, you are not really picky about where you get your nourishment. You take what is easiest to get. Junk food is readily available in the twenty-four hour minimart. It is cheaply made, unhealthy food that comes with a high price tag. The same holds true for emotional hunger. You fall in love with the man who is quick to be interested, who flatters you, and who reminds you how lucky you are to be loved. The men in this scenario fit a particular profile. These men are jealous, controlling, and possessive. Hungry women misinterpret these attributes as love. "He loves me! He can't stand the thought of me talking to another man or even going out with my friends. He thinks I'm so beautiful that men will come on to me. Isn't he wonderful? See how much he loves *me*! If he didn't love me, he wouldn't have fed me chocolate and I wouldn't finally have this wonderful feeling. I know he loves *me*!"

The Abusive Man

As I just noted, the men who know how to give the chocolate, the unhealthy sweetness, fit a particular profile. They too have experienced a childhood that either taught them they have the right to control women, or they have anger at the women who have betrayed them, either mothers or girlfriends. Often they have had fathers who shamed them. (There are plenty of books that adequately describe the characteristics of abusive men, and I won't expand further on the topic here. My focus is on women.) Regardless of the underlying cause, these males grow up with feelings of anger and a need to have power. This male profile is important as it is readily recognized and desired by the emotionally-hungry woman.

If you have chosen abusive men, you are aware—not always consciously, but at an emotional level—that this man "needs" you and you are more than willing to be the one to make up for any childhood hurt or past female betrayal that your man has experienced. You will show him what love really is. You think you know what he needs, although it is your own need you are trying to fulfill. You need to be needed—not wanted, but needed—because if your man *needs* you, he will never leave.

The Need to be "Better Than"

My next discussion will be one that some readers, particularly women who are in a relationship like the one I am about to describe, will find difficult to accept. I expect some women will adamantly deny that race or ethnicity is a factor in their choice of male partners. But to ignore the importance, the history, and the impact of race and ethnicity in the United States would be to deny reality. Over the years of listening to the stories of abuse, I became aware of another feature of abusive relationships. Not all, of course, but many of the stories share a common thread. Emotionally hungry women choose men who are either marginalized by society or men who decide to live on the periphery of society. Many times these women chose men from a different race, ethnicity, or "outside" group. If they choose men from their same culture, race, or ethnicity, they select men who are drug addicted or alcoholics, or men who live on the edge—gang members, criminals, and would-be criminals. Of course I am not saying that men from any one particular race or ethnicity are more inclined to be abusers, addicts, or criminals. What I am saying is that women who choose *abusive* men from groups other than their own do so for a purpose. A woman who chooses a man from a minority group believes, either consciously or unconsciously, that she provides him with "acceptability" and "inclusion" into the larger society. She will choose the insecure, angry man of another race or ethnic group because she believes he needs her to make him whole. She also believes that he feels the same way, and his insecurity and need to be powerful and controlling may be partly due to his conception and understanding of his place in society. These women are not intentionally racist, but their behavior is both condescending and racist. It is a trade-off for both people—acceptance into the majority of society in exchange for never leaving.

The same is true for women who choose abusive, addicted men. They are rescuing the addicts and alcoholics from themselves and their lack of acceptability. How grateful that man should be. He needs a woman to enable him in his addiction or lead him out of it, and the woman believes if he needs her, he will never leave. In all of these examples, the woman gets only a short-term payoff. Steeped in some basic emotional insecurity and desire, she selects someone who is "less than" in order to feel "better than." Unfortunately, that short-term payoff comes with a hefty long-term price of abuse, pain, and repeated loss.

If women are healthy, they are not attracted to and do not need the men who offer the sugar rush. Healthy women have had a lifetime of good emotional health, and although some chocolate is tasty once in a while, healthy women are well aware that a steady diet of sugar will make them sick. Unhealthy, abused women want a steady diet of sugar and chocolate, which only makes them sicker. Women who need the sugar rush have grown up in homes with an emotional diet of oatmeal. Their parents may have kept a roof over their heads and provided clothes and toys, and some may even have been involved in their daughter's lives, going to soccer games and school activities. The crucial point here, however, is not that the parents did these things. It is *why* and *how* they did them. You will learn more about this in chapter nineteen.

8

The Saber-Toothed Tiger

Of all the animals in history, the scariest by far was the saber-toothed tiger. When he stalked his prey, his victim felt a fear so great it paralyzed him and rendered him unable to flee from the huge curved fangs that surely meant death. The real saber-toothed tiger has been extinct for a long time, but I use his name to describe the emotional reality that continues to exist for some women, and that reality is deadly. The saber-toothed tiger is what keeps women from leaving their abusers. The following excerpt from David Kaiser's article (2006), chillingly describes how the Saber-Toothed Tiger stalks and kills the most innocent of victims:

> For 200 years the U.S. government and charitable groups sponsored institutional infanticide, establishments in which unwanted children met early deaths on a daily basis. By the end of the Civil War, 600 institutions of demise were in full swing in the U.S. In Europe the situation was no better. In one gruesome institution in Florence, the Hospital of Innocents, ten thousand infants died before their first birthday. For every three children who passed through these hospital doors two left in a box. Every child in the care of New York institutions died before the age of two, in all but one home. Philadelphia institutions did not have an exceptional home: Every admittant

died. Baltimore institutions fared better; one in ten escaped death through adoption or return to relatives. These institutions of death were known as orphanages. What was killing innocent parentless children? The ultimate infant killing machine: Isolation. Quarantine. Orphanages isolated children from each other and caregivers lest infection spread through human contact, and in so doing, institutionalized neglect spread throughout the modern world (10).

Anyone who has studied psychology is familiar with the work of Harry Harlow, a psychologist who experimented with monkeys to investigate how affection and love influenced development. He created surrogate mothers for his baby primates. Some "mothers" were built and clothed in fabric while others were made of wire. He designed a feeding mechanism for the wire mothers so the babies could feed only from them. He observed that the babies clung to the cloth mothers for much longer periods of time, regardless if they were fed from them. These findings disproved Freud's hypothesis that feeding creates the emotional bond between mother and infant (Brill 1938). There is more to bonding than food. Human babies need a warm, loving mother. *Marasmus* was the original term used to define the phenomenon of infant death that resulted from a lack of affection and emotional closeness. *Marasmus* is a Greek word that means "wasting away." Today the phenomenon is called "failure to thrive." Modern health care and the knowledge now available about the importance of human touch and affection keeps most babies alive today, but psychological implications remain. There is a psychologically meaningful gap that is produced when there is sufficient affection to keep a baby alive, but insufficient affection for the child to emotionally thrive. And

I believe the importance of the psychological impact is vastly overlooked today when it comes to the discussion of women in abusive relationships.

Learning about Loneliness

Now let's return to the lists of childhood feelings and beliefs you wrote earlier and see how they compare with those of other women. I've worked with women from many countries, not just the United States, and I'm convinced that the phenomenon I am about to describe is not cultural. Women from Mexico, Central America, Turkey, England, Morocco, Russia, France, Holland, Japan, and the Middle East have attended my groups. When I ask women to do this exercise, there is one word that almost always tops the list. Regardless of their living situations, family size, socio-economic status, religion, geographic location, race, ethnicity, cultural upbringing, or any other differences in their childhoods, there is one commonality. Their perceptions of childhood are always the same. There is always one enduring similarity—*loneliness*. Was loneliness a word you wrote to describe your childhood? If so, you will understand what I mean. And you may realize how difficult it is to find a word or words that adequately define that feeling.

If you are a reader who has not experienced an abusive relationship, your first reaction to this discussion might be, "All people feel lonely at times, but they don't allow themselves to get beaten up because of it." You're right. However, when I use this word in regard to abused women, I am using it in a different, more profound sense and it isn't easily understood by individuals who have not experienced it. The feelings of loneliness described by abused women are different from the feeling of loneliness other people experience. After many years of working with so many women, I know that a core feeling of unrelenting loneliness is the basis for the fear that prevents women from leaving their abusers. I struggled to find a way to describe it. After doing a good deal of research, it was with much gratitude that I found an article by H. Shmuel Erlich (1998) entitled "On Loneliness, Narcissism and Intimacy." His description is the best I've found to explain the phenomenon I've observed with abused women.

Erlich describes how loneliness is experienced in two different "modalities" that he defines as "Doing" and "Being." In the Doing modality, boundaries are created that provide us with a sense of separateness and distinctiveness from other people. You, in relation to the other, have a different function. In the Doing state, our relationship to others is goal-directed and our thinking is logical. Ending a relationship in the Doing modality would make sense. As I discussed earlier, when a relationship no longer meets the needs of the people involved, or the primary tasks are completed, people leave. A woman operating from a Doing modality would end an abusive relationship because logically she knows that to remain would be dangerous and unhealthy. She might allow her partner to be abusive one or two times, believing the first act was due to unusual circumstances or state of mind, but the second time she would leave. Her clear sense of self would not tolerate harm from another. Upon ending the relationship, the woman may experience loneliness as a feeling of separateness and aloneness, and she would certainly feel apart, both physically and emotionally, from her abuser. She might feel sad and disappointed that her partner did not turn out to be the person she envisioned, but she perceives herself as a separate human being who can continue her life, connecting with others, but with boundaries in place that maintain a sense of self. Erlich writes, "The loneliness experienced in the modality of Doing is the depressive and dejected affect associated with a loss, specifically the loss of the object." In other words, the person feels sad and that sadness is clearly related to the loss of the other person in the relationship. This makes sense. When someone dies or we lose something important to our lives, we feel sad, we grieve, and we move on. Years later we may look back and experience a twinge of melancholy, but our lives go on. Compare this with the following description of loss in the Being modality.

In the Being state, a person experiences merger and fusion between self and another. Thinking, as opposed to logic, is "not geared toward reality testing, precision, and objectivity." It is subjective, and one's existence is related to "connectedness and union with the other. The central experience is thus one of 'being' (hence its name) in fusion and togetherness. There are ... only experiences of 'being' vs. 'non-being.'" A woman who operates from a Being modality experiences the loss of her partner as her "non-being." If he is not in her life, she does not exist. She is or she isn't, there is nothing else, and her connectedness with her partner defines her self. You can see how leaving your partner would be much more emotionally anguishing if to do so would destroy your self. Your fear of obliteration, non-being, would override your fear of being physically hurt or emotionally damaged. Your connection/fusion with your abuser is your very life. Without him you don't exist. There is nothing. You are nothing. *You* cease to exist. Indeed, Erlich states, "The experience of loneliness in this realm does not subscribe to the mode of loss but rather belongs to a gradient of *emptiness* and of *'not being,'* in which (both) subject and object are encompassed without distinction." He goes on to write, "In the Being modality loneliness may be acutely experienced even in the physical presence of the object ..." This is the very example I use when I am working with a woman who is nearing the Saber-Toothed Tiger but hesitates to face reality. Women will say they are afraid of being "alone." There is a difference between being alone and loneliness.

Everyone is alone at some time in his or her life. There probably have been times when you were alone and thoroughly enjoyed it. And there were other times when you were with a group of people and felt lonely, particularly if you've been in an abusive relationship. It seems to go with the territory. When I am working with women in my group and we get to this point of discerning between loneliness and being alone, it is not uncommon for emotional walls to start springing up. I question them about times they have been alone and sometimes they are so set on avoiding the word "lonely" that they emphatically state they have never been alone. I ask if someone always accompanies them to the bathroom. They laugh and finally agree that yes, there are times when they are alone. I ask them if they ever experience a feeling of aloneness when they are with a group of people or with their partner. Each time the answer is yes. In that space the air changes, the tiger looms, we can feel the cold, and I ask again, "What are you afraid will happen if you leave your abuser?" No one wants to say the word. They say, "I'll be alone." But when I clarify the difference between alone and lonely, inevitably there are tears, and with great difficulty the women say, "I'll be lonely." Tears, helplessness, and incredible sadness follow and they concede it is not aloneness, but loneliness, that stalks them in the empty cave of their hearts.

During one of these sessions, one woman said about loneliness, "That word isn't even in my dictionary." Another said, "If I have to feel lonely, I'll jump out the window." Some women are unable to utter the word. Others begin crying and deny that loneliness is an issue. One woman sobbed, "No, it can't be true. Someone has to love me!" These statements are not exaggerations. They convey the deep fear women feel when confronted with reality and the fear of loneliness that is the basis of their need to stay with their abusers.

Again, Erlich describes the feeling that I find abused women trying to express, "some experiential variety of emptiness (apathy, anomie, deadness, lost vitality, disconnectedness, disjointness, petrification, not-being-present) that reflects essentially the experienced 'non-being.'" One of the women

I worked with described her feelings of loneliness as "coming apart." Erlich writes, "It is evident that the loneliness experienced in the sphere of Being is immeasurably more painful and difficult than that encountered in the sphere of Doing." Immeasurably. I can testify to that. It is indescribable.

I ask women, "Tell me three words that describe your childhood." Inevitably, "lonely" is one of the words, and it's uttered with a bowed head, eyes averted, and with sadness and resignation. Sometimes, it's the only word they can find. There is a visceral awareness that they are about to enter the lair of the saber-toothed tiger—a fearful, sad, empty, desolate place. Reality denies this woman-child a place of security, caring, welcome, and love. She has no emotional home.

If you wrote loneliness as one of your words, or the primary word, to describe your childhood, right now you are probably crying or on the verge of tears. You know the feeling I am trying to describe. You acknowledge the emptiness, the awful loneliness that feels as if you are dying and realize that any hope you had to fill the void does not exist. It feels as if your heart is bleeding life and your soul is dying. You are saying goodbye after the long struggle to matter, to become visible. There is nothing more. There is only you, alone and lonely. A feeling so frightening you are willing to risk your life to avoid it. Now you can no longer deny the reality of the Saber-Toothed Tiger, of your life and your love.

Loneliness to a healthy person feels different from that experienced by an invisible child, an abused woman. For the healthy person, it is transitory. It will eventually go away. If you are an abused woman, loneliness is unbearable and unrelenting. Again, you are cognitively aware that your fear appears to be unreasonable, silly, or crazy, but the fear is also very real and very strong and the emotional impact drives your behavior. Let us begin to figure out how to heal.

9

Growing Up with the Saber-Toothed Tiger

Returning to Erlich's work, he asserts, "Developmentally speaking, in my view, both these modalities begin their influence from the onset of life. There is increasing evidence that the newborn infant is equipped and functions from the start with *both* an acute, sharply differentiated capacity for reality assessment, based on the infant's inherent separateness from his mother, and also with a capacity for fusion and merger with her." It is my belief that women who become involved with abusive men operate from a "Being modality" created at birth and reinforced throughout their childhoods—in other words, emotional oatmeal.

Let's return to your second list of messages you received during childhood. Sometimes women's lists include the words *stupid, ugly, fat, skinny, worthless, incapable, useless, never good enough, never expected to amount to anything, less than*, and so on. You get the picture. Perhaps your list contains the same or similar words. These are straightforward messages and you know how damaging they can be when they are believed. Sometimes, however, the messages get sent in another way—through indifference. Women who grew up with indifferent parents relate they felt invisible. No matter how hard they tried, no one noticed, and they usually reacted in a similar way: *Maybe if I just try harder, get better grades, look prettier, or score the winning goal, they will notice me and love me and I won't feel so left out. I won't feel this loneliness.* The messages these little girls received were not negative. No one ever called them names or belittled them. They just didn't receive any feedback about their performance in life. However, no feedback sends a meta-message and it says, "We're not interested." It is hard for a child to understand why the parents, who matter so much to the child, don't respond in kind. Of course, these thoughts are not conscious. There is no internal dialogue about why one's parents aren't terribly interested. What does occur is a consistent sense of being invisible, transparent, and unnoticed.

The message does not have to be intentional and parents may even be well-meaning. One woman related that throughout her childhood, her mother always said, "You can do better." Regardless of her achievement or effort, the response from her mother was the same. The same message was also sent to her brother, so in her case, it did not involve different expectations based on gender. Her mother wanted her children to do better in life than she had, and her intention was to encourage them to always do their best. However, my client interpreted the message to say that her performance in all ways was never good enough. She was not perfect and anything short of perfection was inadequate.

Whichever way the message is sent, deliberately or unintentionally, it is interpreted negatively by the recipient. They feel unimportant, not good enough, unlovable, unwanted, or invisible. At this point you might say we have returned to the topic of low self-esteem, but remember, the women had sufficient belief in themselves to make significant achievements in various areas of their lives. They may have received negative messages from others in their lives, friends or acquaintances, but chose not to believe or internalize those messages. It is not so much the content of the message itself that is important but the *person* who sends the message. And the most important person in your life at birth is your primary caregiver, which in most cases is your mother, or a mother-figure. I hate to sound Freudian and blame mothers for all our problems, but I would be remiss if I did not report what I have learned and what I know to be true in the case of abused women.

In cases where there is physical and/or sexual abuse from a parent or caretaker, the effect of indifference to the child is underscored, but in and of itself, this type of abuse is not sufficient to create the loneliness I am describing. The girl who is raped by her father or stepfather, and whose mother believes her and intervenes to protect her daughter, sends a different message than the mother who disbelieves and allows the assaults to continue. Many women experience sexual abuse as children but as adults do not tolerate physical abuse from their partners. Although childhood sexual abuse is far too common, it is not a prerequisite for, nor does it explain why, some women end up in abusive relationships. The same holds true for childhood physical abuse. A history of childhood abuse is often used by women to explain why they are presently abused, but again this fulfills their need to find an explanation; it's not the real reason they are in an abusive relationship. Many women who never experienced childhood physical or sexual abuse are in abusive relationships. It is obvious that this is not the explanation for the abusive relationship they are in today, or the intense loneliness that endures. Although some research indicates that exposure to violence during childhood can be associated with increased rates of violence in one's marital relationship, it also demonstrates what makes a difference. "Studies that have examined mediating factors in the intergenerational transmission of violence suggest that the cycle of violence is less likely to repeat itself if the child had the nurturance, love and support of at least one parent ..." (Chibucos and Leite 2005, 102). Again, the importance of love, even if only from one person (ideally a parent), is vital, and especially so in the lives of females.

Just as childhood sexual and/or physical abuse is not necessary to impart these intense feelings of loneliness, neither are there other particular definable experiences.

Instead the loneliness appears to derive from a process that includes how one interpreted and reacted to childhood experiences. It is important to point out that in some cases, there is no one particular person to blame. However, in other cases, it is very clear who is to blame. Based on my experience working with abused women, parents send both intentionally and unintentionally clear messages to their daughters. In any case, the child's need for love, attention, and security are not met. Let's return to Janet's story as an example.

"I guess you'd say ours was what's called a traditional family. Daddy worked in a factory and Mother stayed home. It was unseemly in those days for women to have to work outside the home. Mother was the best housekeeper, a really good cook, and she taught herself to oil paint. She was a good artist. People always commented on it. Daddy worked awful hard and he was proud, brought his paycheck home every week. We had food on the table, a roof over our heads, and decent—not the best—but decent clothes. There was no physical punishment—we just knew how we were expected to behave."

Although there was no physical or sexual abuse in the home, there were some traditional family beliefs that undermined Janet's sense of welcome in the world. Janet was the fourth daughter and she was born only fourteen months after the birth of her older sister. This configuration takes on special meaning when we look at the family history.

"My mother had four sisters and only one brother. Her brother was killed in an accident when he was young. Daddy had two sisters and he only had one brother, too. My uncle didn't have any children so Daddy always said he was the only one who could carry on the family name. My father was always working, didn't do much with us girls, but when my little brother was born that was sure a change. I think they liked my oldest sisters. You know, they were the first ones so they got attention. Then my older sister came along and I was born fourteen months later and I just know we were terrible disappointments. I just feel it. One of us was supposed to be a boy. I know Mother must have been so busy; there was no such thing as 'quality time.' My oldest sister was no joy either. She made fun of me, told me how dumb and ugly I was. Like I said, things changed when my brother was born. It was like the sun rose every day on that child. Daddy brought home presents for him, took him on walks through the park. I could tell Mother was happy too, like she finally did something she'd been trying to do for a long time. I felt like I just disappeared. They were always taking pictures of my brother. Don't get me wrong; I love my brother, but I was so hungry for attention. I just got lost in the crowd."

Families often want male heirs, so Janet's family was not unusual in this regard. In this type of family, a lack of, or loss of, male children increases the value of sons. Janet's parents were not malicious people, and they didn't intentionally send a message of disappointment. After all, they were young, busy parents who were doing the best they could; but Janet got the message. They didn't have to tell her she was not wanted. She knew it with her first breath. She hoped in her own childish way that it was untrue, but over the years it could no longer be denied, especially when her mother said, during some casual discussion about birth control, "Well, I never wanted you." Hope that she really was wanted and loved not only died, it crashed and burned.

If Janet had been welcomed into the world and experienced physical and emotional affection during her childhood, her reaction to her mother's words would have been different. She may have laughed and easily accepted that many children are conceived accidentally. If your birth is not planned but you are lovingly welcomed into the family, you feel it. And if your birth is not planned, you are not welcomed, and there is an absence of physical affection, you feel that too. Throughout her life, Janet has had dreams of walking among groups of people in malls, schools, and work situations, where she is barely acknowledged by others. She feels invisible, always on the periphery. Her dreams are sad and scary—dreams of emptiness and disconnection. Janet's dreams express the enduring loneliness that results from a childhood bereft of essential love.

10

The Value of Loneliness

What is the value of loneliness? Why would human beings experience such a difficult and scary emotion? It is reasonable to think that all aspects of human development occurred to help us, as a species, to survive. Therefore loneliness must have a purpose. When humans lived in caves, a lone person would not have survived for long. In a world where large, dangerous animals roamed, humans were vulnerable prey. A man might be able to hunt and gather food, but if he became sick or injured, who would care for him until he was strong enough to hunt again? Likewise, women with babies would need someone to provide food for them and protect them from dangerous animals. The tribe or clan members needed one another for survival. They were interdependent, the same as modern humans, but today's needs are different. In prehistoric times, being alone in the cave was scary because being alone meant you were going to die. There was a good chance the saber-toothed tiger would find and eat you. Being alone was connected with certain death and gave rise to feelings of fear and vulnerability. The repeated scary experience translated to a survival emotion—loneliness compelled humans to seek out others—a definite survival skill.

Loneliness is not to be taken lightly. In most countries, people who break the law are isolated from the rest of society by placement in prisons. And within prisons, how are convicts punished if they don't follow the rules? They're sent to solitary confinement. Prisoners of war experience the same thing. Their captors isolate them from their comrades in order to break them down and gain control. Some religious sects punish sinners within their groups through a practice called "shunning," where members in good standing are directed not to talk to, or in any way acknowledge, the offender. This practice effectively isolates the person, and the emotional pain that results motivates the offender to change behavior and adhere to the beliefs of the community. Humans have always found that removing an offender from their midst and creating a state of isolation is an effective way of maintaining social mores and bringing people in line. Ask any junior high girl how it feels when she has been ostracized by her peers because she doesn't have just the right kind of clothes or has offended the group in some way. Creating the sense of isolation and loneliness is a well-known and used method of punishment. It hurts both psychologically and emotionally.

Although loneliness evolved to keep people together for survival purposes, like the tailbone and appendix, its usefulness isn't as evident anymore, and perhaps it isn't as necessary. After all, now we can go to the twenty-four hour mini-mart and get a burger at midnight if we're hungry, or have a pizza delivered right to our caves. If we hurt ourselves, we call 911 and someone comes to take us to the emergency room. We still need each other's skills, but we don't necessarily have to live in the same cave and crouch around the same fire in order to survive. Now we can choose with whom we share the fire. When healthy women feel lonely, they can call Mom and Dad, friends or lovers, and again feel cared about and loved. They're just experiencing a little of that old leftover feeling from eons ago.

It isn't the same for unwanted, unloved, emotionally-neglected girls who grow up to be abused women. The unwanted baby grows in the womb with an ungodly twin who follows her birth and nourishes itself on the flesh of her heart and the breath of her soul. Loneliness isn't a twinge or a pang that goes away with a little extra human contact. Loneliness to this woman has the same meaning as death, the Saber-Toothed Tiger's hot breath on her face, his fangs bared to slice the jugular. To some readers this may sound exaggerated. I assure you it is not.

The unwanted baby knows from the first day of life, maybe even before, she is not cherished or loved. She is held and fed, but it is a duty or a chore, or the right thing to do after doing the same for siblings born before her. No sense of being special is conveyed to this kid—she's just there and the message is clear, "I really don't want you."

Still-Face

At this point you may be doubtful that loneliness has such a profound and long-lasting effect on children, particularly to the extent that when they grow to be women they would allow themselves to endure incredible abuse in order to avoid any exposure to it. However, research supports this fact. In 1978 an experiment was designed to study how babies respond to their mothers' facial expressions, and how babies react when they do not get their mothers' attention (Tronick et. al. 1978). In this study, a mother and child interacted while being videotaped using two cameras and a split-screen monitor. The baby was soothed and placed in a comfortable reclining carrier in a curtained area where there would be no distraction and the baby could focus only on its mother's face. The mother sat facing her infant and played with the baby for three minutes. Following the play session, the mother left the area for thirty seconds then returned and again sat across from the infant. However, for the next three-minute session the mother was to present with a neutral, expressionless face—a still face. Altogether seven infants, from two to twenty weeks of age, and their mothers participated in the study. The researchers studied the videotapes and carefully noted how the infants reacted to both the play and still-face sessions. They observed vocalizations, facial expression and movement, head position, body posture, and direction of gaze. The authors state, "The effect of the violation of reciprocity in the still-face condition can be seen clearly in the contrast between the infant's behavior during a normal interaction and the same infant's behavior during the experimental condition" (1978, 5). The infant's behavior during a normal interactive session was characterized by expectant looks toward the mother, smiles, body oriented to mother, hand, arm, and leg movements toward the mother, vocalizations and a "beseeching" look into her face when she stops her playful actions. As the mother prepares to leave the cubicle, "his mouth turns down, his eyebrows arch, his legs and arms quiet, and he follows her with his eyes and head as she moves away" (1978, 7). The infant was clearly enjoying his mother's attention and was aware that she was leaving and the fun was over.

Compare that description to how the baby reacted during the still-face period. When the mother entered the curtained area and wore an expressionless face, the baby attempted to get her attention by smiling and glancing toward her, but appeared wary and concerned. After several failed attempts to gain a response the infant's expression became serious and, "he completely withdraws, his body curled over, his head down. He does not look again at his mother …. He looks wary, helpless, and withdrawn. As the mother exits … he looks halfway up in her direction, but his sober facial expression and his curled body position do not change … this description illustrates the typical pattern of an infant's response to his mother remaining still-faced" (1978, 8).

The Still-Face effect has been studied and replicated for more than twenty years. Additional research has introduced adult touch to the experiments and found that touch is a powerful reinforcement for young infants (Muir and Lee 2003, 484). I wrote earlier that I believe that babies know from birth if they are welcomed, wanted, and loved. The research shows that infants are motivated to engage with others, are well-attuned to others, and are highly sensitive to how others interact with them (Striano 2004). An infant's expectation of reciprocal interaction with mother is clearly established by four weeks of age and may be evident as early as two to three weeks (Tronick et al. 1978). What is most disturbing about the findings of the still-face experiments is how quickly an infant becomes distressed when her mother emotionally withdraws. "The still-face mothers in our study remained unresponsive for only 3 minutes, yet their infants found even such a temporary violation greatly disturbing" (1978, 12). In his later research, Tronick found, "These reactions occur even when the mothers are still-faced for only a few seconds" (1989, 114). He further states:

> Clearly, the emotional state of others is of fundamental importance to the infant's emotional state ... Of course, an infant could completely give up the goal of engaging his or her mother. However, the young infant may not be able to give up this goal, and even if he or she could, the consequences might be even more severe (Bowlby 1982) ... The infant gives up attempting to appreciate the nature of the immediate situation and instead approaches new situations already withdrawn and biased to act inappropriately. This severely constricts the infant's engagement with the world, future options, and even autonomy and may lead to failure-to thrive, depression, and other forms of infant psychopathology ... Certainly the way in which the adult-as-child regulated and represented the circumstances and the emotions he or she experienced accrue to the adult (1989, 117–118).

I agree. The infant, the young child, the teenager, the woman cannot give up the goal of wanting to be visible, loved, and touched. Tronick provides one of the most striking descriptions of an infant's reaction to the Still-Face and subsequent inability to elicit a response: "The infant experiences a feeling of 'shrinking'" (2003, 479). This is an apt description of loneliness in the "Being" state, again a feeling of not-being, disappearing, invisibility.

The Still-Face studies plainly demonstrate the distress babies feel when they are invisible even for a brief time. Imagine how that feels, and the emotional consequences that occur, when you are invisible the moment you are born, every day, most of the time, for all of the days of your childhood. That's a lot of oatmeal.

Erich Fromm, in his timeless book *The Art of Loving*, describes the ideal experience for an infant who is loved and the hopelessness of a child who is not:

> *I am loved*. I am loved because I am mother's child ... I am loved because I am beautiful, admirable ... *I am loved for what I am*, or perhaps more accurately, *I am loved because I am* ... There is nothing I have to do in order to be loved—mother's love is unconditional. All I have to do is to *be*—to be her child. Mother's love is bliss, is peace, it need not be acquired, it need not be deserved. But there is a negative side, too, to the unconditional quality of mother's love. Not only does it not need to be deserved—it also *cannot* be acquired, produced, controlled. If it is there, it is like a blessing; if it is not there, it is as if all beauty had gone out of life—and there is nothing I can do to create it (1956, 33).

Each individual comes into the world completely dependent on the care and competence of another human being. A mother and father might be too young, too old, too poor, too rich, too stoned, too drunk, too stressed, too mentally unstable, too sick, too busy, too lazy, too stupid, too smart, too burdened, too tired, too manic, too depressed, too hungry, too scared, too lonely. Unfortunately, an innocent child's life is in their hands. Fortunately, there is that big chunk of people that fall in the "average" range on the bell curve. Also, fortunately, humans have (thanks to the Saber-Toothed Tiger) an inherent survival drive that includes a mechanism that motivates parents to love and care for helpless infants. Thus human life continues, despite all the frailties of humanity. Also, fortunately, again thanks to the Saber-Toothed Tiger, humans have partners, families, clans, tribes, societies, and cultures that lend themselves to support and teach new parents the skills needed to nurture helpless infants.

Where does the healing begin? It would be wonderful if every parent-to-be and every parent of a young child could simply read this book and realize the importance of loving and welcoming their children and then change their behavior accordingly. I doubt that will happen, but I can hope.

I believe the initial love and welcoming into the world has to come from the mother. In the animal kingdom, babies and mothers recognize one another by smell, and it is a rarity when one animal nurses another's offspring. There is some evidence to indicate the same identification process occurs with humans. Even if a baby is taken from her mother at birth and handed to a loving adoptive parent, something is still missing. It is possible that something doesn't "smell" right and that might result in something not "feeling" right to the child. I don't believe this scenario is sufficient to predispose a girl to grow up and become involved in abusive relationships. But I am proposing that in some cases, there may be a biological component to the process. Indeed, if the adoptive parents are affectionate and loving, the child may overcome the initial loss of the biological mother and grow up to be a healthy woman. If the adoptive parents are too busy or too involved with other matters and the child's need for love is not met, the child may become doubly vulnerable and attracted to abusive partners.

Emotional Neglect

Severe damage is done by mothers and caregivers who intentionally send the message of "not loved" to their daughters, and who allow them to be physically and/or sexually abused. And just as much damage is done by sending the "not loved" message through emotional neglect. In his book *The Relationship Cure,* John Gottman describes how we all seek to be acknowledged and connect with others. He calls our attempts to connect "bidding." Bids to connect can be verbal statements or questions, or they might be nonverbal; for example, facial expressions, playful and affectionate touching, and caring gestures, such as handing someone a glass or opening a door. Regardless of what form they take, the desired outcome is to have another person acknowledge and respond to us. There are three ways that people respond to one another's bids for attention. "Turning toward" occurs when one person in the relationship makes a bid for attention and the other responds in a positive manner. For example, a child asks her mother for a cookie. It doesn't matter in this context whether the answer is yes or no. It is the manner of response that is important. Mother might say, "Not right now. It's almost dinnertime." Or she might say, "Yes, but be sure to eat all your dinner." Either way, she has turned toward her child and acknowledged the bid for attention—the child is visible.

Another way to respond to a bid for attention is "turning against." Using the same example of the child asking for a cookie, an angry turning against response would be, "Why are you always bothering me? Can't you leave me alone for one minute? Go play!" Turning against is a hostile response, but it still informs the child that she is visible. She has been heard. It would seem that a turning against response would be very damaging, and it is, but not to the extent of "turning away."

When a parent responds to a child's bid for attention by turning away, there is no acknowledgement of the child. She is ignored, or the response is unrelated to the bid. Again, the little girl asks for a cookie. Her mother does not respond verbally or even look at the child. The girl is entirely invisible. An example of an unrelated response is, "Go see what your brother is doing." The child is invisible for who *she* is although she is visible for the needs and demands of someone else. She sees herself as unimportant to the one person she needs the most—the person responsible for keeping her alive. Gottman describes the negative effects that occur when there is persistent turning away. "When somebody turns away from a bid, the bidder loses confidence and self-esteem … they just seem to fold in on themselves" (2001, 47). And he asserts the effects are particularly damaging to children. "In children the effects can be worse. Kids look to their mothers and fathers for emotional cues. They need their parents to validate their feelings and guide them. When parents fail to do this, kids begin to doubt themselves. They begin to feel lonely in their emotions, internalizing problems and wondering, 'What's wrong with me that I feel this way?'" (2001, 47)

An interesting study by Prem Fry, Research Professor at Trinity Western University, and Lisa A. Barker, Counselor (2002), was conducted to examine social support networks for women survivors of domestic violence. The women in the study identified those who provided support either emotionally, financially, and practically, by giving advice or by socializing. Eighty-five percent of the participants identified close friends as the most satisfying members of their support group. Co-workers and hired professionals (counselors and attorneys) constituted 60 percent and 38 percent, respectively. Where are the parents? In the bottom 10 percent category, and they were identified as providing financial and practical support, not emotional support. The authors conclude, "It is conceivable that participants in the present study perceived less support coming from the family because they had higher expectations of family members ... lower satisfaction with the support from family members may be that because of the longstanding bond with family members, a victim of violence may feel a greater sense of dismay, hurt, and betrayal when parents and family members do not provide support unconditionally and readily" (2002, 156). I contend that women are dissatisfied with parental support because they are too well aware that their parents were never emotionally supportive to begin with, and they know better than to risk that invisibility again.

Of course, no parent is perfect and we all make mistakes when raising children, just as our parents made mistakes with us, and theirs before them. Parents who genuinely love their children will convey it and the child will know, regardless of the mistakes that are made along the way—every bid for attention and affection does not have to be met with "turning toward." It is the ongoing, grinding down, wearing away, the deep loneliness of the "turning away" that leaves the child in the lonely cave with the Saber-Toothed Tiger, the death sentence of despair.

I want to clarify and underscore that it isn't about blaming, it's about understanding. You must learn why you ended up in an abusive situation, accept the reality of your childhood, change how you perceive yourself, and give yourself the love you need. You have survived through your own hope, intellect, determination, anger, altruism, fear, or perhaps even by accident. No matter how it happened, you have survived. You already have the foundation you need to become the strongest person you know.

11

Dear Old Dad

A number of women I've counseled have reported that their mothers were unloving, but they had special relationships with their fathers. They were sure their fathers loved them. For example, Wendy had two children, a good job in a doctor's office, and a nice house. She worked hard to support herself and her children after she left her abusive boyfriend. It was her second abusive relationship. The first was with her husband, the father of her children. She came to counseling wondering how she ever got involved with another abuser. Wendy appeared tired, as if the effort to keep going was getting to be more than she could handle. She was slightly overweight and her clothes were dark and baggy. It was hard to tell where her long dark hair ended and her clothing began. Wendy told me that she loved her father, who was "always there for me."

"My mother wasn't like my dad. She was always yelling at me, putting me down, and if I stepped out of line one time, she'd haul off and hit me. Sometimes it was worse than that. Mom worked a lot and I was the one who had to keep the house, cook, do everything, and take care of my little brothers and sisters. It got so bad with my mom. One time she got so mad she came after me with a kitchen knife. She said she was going to cut my face up and she was running toward me. The little kids were in the house too, but it didn't matter to her. I ran out of the house and stayed at a friend's place and that was it for me. I was never going back."

I asked about her father. "My father didn't work so much. I'm not sure why now. It just seemed like he was home more, and I would fix him coffee and we'd sit on the porch and talk. He was kind, never yelled at any of us. He'd listen to me. I enjoyed our time sitting together. I loved him."

When I asked where he was when her mother was verbally or physically abusive, Wendy replied that he was home, sometimes in the other room. I asked if her mother yelled loudly. "Oh, yes, sometimes the neighbors complained," she replied. I asserted that indeed her father could also hear the yelling. At this point, there was a look of surprise on Wendy's face. I asked if her father had ever intervened to stop the abuse. For the first time in her life, Wendy became aware that her father was not innocent. He chose to allow the abuse. He stayed in the other room and washed his hands of it. Wendy had taken the place of her mother, providing emotional comfort to her father. In doing so, she felt wanted and needed and she also learned that a semblance of love could be earned if necessary. However, Wendy's giving and caring was, in reality, a one-way street. With the realization that her father could have and should have stopped the abuse, Wendy saw the truth of his selfishness and indifference. More deeply, she knew he, too, did not love her. He used her. The vacant place carved from the lack of a parent's love cannot be filled with substitutes or lies.

Sometimes a mother or father leaves the family and no longer has interaction with the child. Usually one parent leaves as a result of divorce or the parents never married and the relationship ended before or shortly after the child is born. Frequently, women believe that the absent parent actually loves them and if it weren't for the remaining parent interfering, the absent parent would be attentive, loving, and involved. I encourage women to look for evidence with their own children. Would they be able to leave their children? If not, why not? I find that women who have experienced unloving childhoods want to deeply love their own children. They consciously make every effort to ensure that their own children know they are loved. They do not want to pass on to their children the lonely feelings they carry from their childhood. I ask them to explain how it is possible that an absent parent could leave in the first place. Wouldn't a father try everything possible to see his child if he loved her? Where is the evidence of love? All too often, it is evident that the absent parent really didn't care about her either, and she has been holding on to a dream of someone loving her. When a parent leaves a child with little or no attempt to communicate, the message is the same for the child: "I don't care enough to try and see you. I don't love you." When this happens to a little girl who already feels unwanted, it further accentuates her feelings of fear and loss.

Some girls receive very clear messages that they are not cared for if they are being sexually abused. If sexual abuse occurs, she learns that sexuality will bring her attention. Her body may not always belong to her and she may be aware that it is being used, but sexual interaction is still attention and the girl may learn and eventually choose to use her sexuality to gain attention as a form of affection. Young women may become sexually promiscuous in their search for visibility. Being touched is an acknowledgment of one's existence. Readers are probably familiar with the dynamic between pimp and prostitute. The pimp showers his "girls" with attention, gifts, and "love." He wants them to feel special, and as a result, they are devoted to him. He can also be cruel and abusive, yet the prostitute will endure being debased in order to maintain the relationship. It isn't about money. It is about filling the emptiness of childhood. It's about fending off the Saber-Toothed Tiger, and the pimp is the ultimate abuser because he understands the tiger. A pimp may even believe his behavior is commendable. After all, he's giving the woman something she desperately needs. He's better than her parents. Better than all the other men in her life. He knows her, knows her need, and that is more than anyone has taken the time to realize. The Saber-Toothed Tiger is a pimp's best friend.

For the unwanted and unloved child, loneliness actually means death. If you were unwanted and unloved, you knew at any given time your parents would rather you not be there. As a new baby you sensed you were an intrusion, and you experienced feelings of rejection and disapproval. Just by being born you created anger, unhappiness, resentment, disappointment, and/or indifference in the very people you needed the most. Enough was given to keep you alive, and you learned this, too. You probably made a great effort to improve or get attention, to become visible. "Please love me. Let me live. I'll try harder. Let me live. I'll be smarter (or dumber, taller, thinner, faster, prettier). Let me live. Please approve of me. Please, please love *me*! Please, please, let me live." The Saber-Toothed Tiger breathed down your neck all through your childhood. He was your constant fearful companion. You walked with the cruelest death everyday. You had no clan that cared.

Until you read this book, you may not have been consciously aware of the pervasive feeling of loneliness, and you may not have connected them to your relationship with your mother or primary caregiver. And I'm sure you didn't connect your lonely childhood to your choice of an abusive partner. Or maybe you are one of the women who are very aware of being unwanted and unloved. Your childhood experience might range from parental neglect, resignation, indifference, or minimal caring to rejection, outright hostility, or physical and sexual abuse. Perhaps you are one of the women who emphasizes that certainly you know your mother loved you. If so, look for the evidence. Again, not words, but hard facts. I doubt you will recall a childhood of loneliness if you had felt loved. This may be the first time you actually look at your childhood and your relationship with your mother. There is a strong need to believe you were loved and wanted because that means your mother would protect, feed, and clothe you. She would shelter and comfort you. She would not let you die, physically or emotionally.

There are other reasons why parents take care of their children. Note, I said "take care" instead of "care for." It does not occur to some women that their parents took care of them because, "What would the neighbors think?" if they hadn't. Parents may feel a moral obligation, or simply be resigned to the fact that this is what life has given them. These parents often resent their children but feel guilty about feeling resentful. They don't say it in words. Instead they communicate resignation or resentment through a lack of affection, attention, and love. Children get the message early, "We really don't want you, but we'll take care of you (at least at the minimal oatmeal level) because we have to. We're not happy about you. In fact, we're angry, resentful, or resigned that you're here. So please, just eat your oatmeal and stay out of the way. We're busy making a living, or taking care of the siblings, or building a career, or looking for our own sugar rush, or whatever it is that certainly is more important than you. Most of all, don't ask us to love you. That's *way* too much to ask."

From a child's viewpoint, adults are the people who are supposed to know everything. They know who deserves to be loved and who does not. They have to be right. They're the big people. Little girls who are not loved and held and nurtured emotionally grow up to be emotionally-hungry women. When one grows up without love, there doesn't seem to be enough love in the whole world to satisfy the emptiness—a hollow void of the heart that can never be filled.

Girls who are sexually abused don't misinterpret abuse as affection. Girls know they are not truly cared for and loved if they are hurt and exploited. They know it's not about them. Being held and loved occurs in a healthy, caring way, with a focus on the child's needs, not the needs of a selfish adult. The same holds true for the adult who appears involved in a girl's life, but actually needs to have a child who is successful, popular, or athletic. The child is used as a pawn to meet the parent's needs. Children aren't stupid. They may not always have the words or education to communicate their feelings, but they know how being "unloved" feels. It feels invisible.

12

Hunger

One day, while paying for groceries at the checkout counter, the clerk remarked about my late shopping hour and I replied I had just finished working. She asked about my work, and I told her I had conducted two counseling groups that evening. A discussion ensued about counseling and my work with women who have experienced abuse. She said, "Women like that have just never been loved, so they think that's what love is." I let the conversation drop. She was partially right, but it's not that simple. Remember, abused women come from all walks of life and are neither stupid nor naïve. It is insulting to think they have no concept or experience of love. They know full well that love is not abuse and that abuse is wrong. They may have been loved by healthy men, even married them. They may have been able to have a long marriage without abuse if it weren't for the incessant craving to fill their inner emptiness. Frequently a woman comes to counseling while she's presently involved in a terribly abusive marriage. She may have had several such relationships, and when asked if she's had any relationships that were not abusive, she may have had one that she finds unexplainable. Often these "healthy" relationships are described as boring, passionless, or there was just something missing. It isn't that she doesn't know what love is. Instead, because of the life-long hunger, a healthy relationship feels like oatmeal, entirely emotionally unsatisfying. When you grow up with the Saber-Toothed Tiger panting at your back, you long for safety. Extreme loneliness carves out a space in your inner being that hungers for a kind touch, a loving word, a look that conveys genuine awareness of one's being. The hunger is constant. You can try to fill the emptiness with a large bank account, a list of accomplishments, or making sure you don't have an empty minute in your day, but the hunger is never satisfied with substitutes. It can only be sated with love—genuine, sincere love.

Your interpretation and definition of your childhood is based on these feelings of extreme loneliness, and the yearning for visibility drives you to the decisions you make when selecting abusive men. If you have married and had children, it might surprise you that the emptiness remains. It is the void, the hunger for unconditional love, that only a loving mother or caregiver can provide. Due to the deprivation from which it arose, your hunger is extreme. "Skin hunger" is a term that describes the need for human touch. Women frequently report they experienced little or no physical affection from their parents and certainly, that is a part of the hunger. The women I have worked with relate entire childhoods bereft of any hugging, sitting on someone's lap, being tucked into bed, goodnight kisses, and rarely, if ever, an "I love you." Others have heard the words but the treatment they received didn't match. It was conditional on their performance or a parent's mood or sobriety.

Let's return to Janet's story.

"Sundays were quiet days at our house. Mother would fix breakfast and everybody would read the Sunday paper. Mother, my closest sis, and I would all sit in the big chair. I called it the 'fuzzy chair' because it was one of those overstuffed ones. I was too young and didn't know how to read yet. Mother would read the comics to us. I don't ever remember being touched when I was little, never hugged, never told I was loved. I still remember how it felt to sit in that big chair, me on one side and sis on the other, and Mother reading and pointing to the pictures. It was the closest I could be to my mother. I wanted so badly to have her put her arm around me. I just ached for her. It never happened. Eventually, I guess we outgrew sitting in the chair. When I shut my eyes I can feel how it was and how I wanted a hug so bad. One time, I was about seven years old and I had a friend, Mary. We would play beauty shop. It wasn't much, that's for sure. She had a hair brush and I'd sit on the curb and she would brush my hair. She liked my long brown hair and she would brush it and put it up on top of my head. It felt so wonderful. Someone was touching me in a warm, kind way. It felt delicious and I've never forgotten that. I'll always love Mary for that memory. I wish it had been my mother's touch."

Other women have told me similar stories. Melody, who you met earlier, recalled how during a family reunion when she was three years old, she wandered around the neighborhood while her family visited in a relative's home. Darkness fell and no one called her or asked after her. She watched the lighted windows from a distance and wandered to the house long after dark. No one showed concern. That experience and many similar ones, along with plenty of "you are unloved" messages, convinced Melody that it didn't matter if she lived or died. No one cared.

Rosa, another woman who came to my groups, related how she was treated by her grandmother after her mother died when she was five years old and went to live with her. Rosa was made to clean the house, given very little food to eat, and was left naked on the floor to sleep. She was told she was lazy and didn't deserve food or clothes. Rosa received extreme messages about being unwanted.

In contrast, Sylvia's life was quite different. Her parents were financially well-off and they were quite active in all of Sylvia's school and extracurricular activities, but they were busy. On the surface it would appear they were average loving parents. However, children are not fooled by appearances. Sylvia knew the real reason her parents participated in her activities. When parents love their children and take part because they want children to know they are loved, the children know it and feel loved. A different message is sent when parents do all the activities because it is what society or the people in their social class or neighborhood expect them to do. Sylvia's parents were not concerned with how well Sylvia was doing. They wanted to ensure that they were perceived as "involved" parents. Even at a young age, Sylvia knew this, although not consciously. Adding to the awareness that she was not valued for her own sake—for who she was as their child—Sylvia also had a babysitter who made cruel remarks about her being overweight and stupid. With no readily available parent to disprove these remarks, Sylvia grew up believing she was "not good enough" and she hungered for approval. These examples are just a few of the hundreds of very similar stories I've heard from abused women.

My theory that infant/childhood loneliness is the absolute reason why women are attracted to and stay with abusive men is convincingly validated by a young woman named Sheryl. Initially she did not seem to have the same experience of emotional neglect in her childhood that is typical of other women who have been abused. Both her mother and father were professionals who Sheryl described as supportive, loving parents. Although Sheryl and her father did not always see eye to eye, she knew he loved her. Sheryl and her mother were close and enjoyed a healthy mother-daughter relationship. She could not recall ever having a sense that her parents did not want and not welcome her, particularly because she was their only child. They adopted Sheryl after years of trying to have a child, and they were happy to finally bring a baby into their home. Despite what looked like a healthy, loving family, Sheryl was involved with a physically abusive man by the time she was twenty-three. She lived with him for three years, and after enduring many incidences of severe abuse, one of which caused her to fear for her life, she knew she had to leave. Her parents welcomed her back home and encouraged her to stay with them as long as she needed. When she came to me for counseling a year after she left the relationship, Sheryl was still having difficulty saying goodbye and ending contact with her abuser. He continued to call her and tried to convince her to return to him. Sheryl felt more distress after each conversation.

As Sheryl and I explored her childhood, I could not find a reason why she was so afraid of letting go of her abuser. She related an ordinary childhood that she described as happy and loving, but *lonely*. The lonely feelings she reported didn't fit with the way she portrayed her childhood. Why would a child who was loved and wanted, and shown affection and care, feel lonely? It was not until we had spent a number of sessions together that Sheryl reported that she had talked with her mother and discovered she had not been adopted at birth as originally believed. She had been taken from her birth mother and placed in a foster home for three months prior to being adopted. This is significant with regard to the evidence in the Still Face studies, which indicates children at this very early age become distressed when ignored. Neither Sheryl nor I could know the circumstances she experienced in foster care. Was the foster mother overly busy with other children and unable to provide the emotional connection Sheryl needed in order to experience a feeling of safety? Perhaps the foster mother did not want to interact emotionally because she knew this little baby would be leaving her and she did not want to become attached to her. Whatever the case may have been, I am convinced that those three months were crucial to the development of fear and loneliness that Sheryl eventually carried with her throughout her life. Sheryl knew, as all children know, when she was not welcomed—when the still face of death, not-being, invisibility looked away from her and left her with the emptiness of the Saber-Toothed Tiger, the loneliness.

Beginning to Heal

Once you recognize the source of the hunger and loneliness, the healing can begin. It does not begin with looking for another partner to end the loneliness. It begins with providing the missing love to yourself. When you grow up hungry, there isn't enough love in the outside world to fill the emptiness. You might marry or engage in a relationship, but it is as if you can completely absorb all of the emotions the other person has to share and you will still not be satisfied. Your partner cannot possibly fill the void. Only the mother/caregiver can provide the type of unconditional love that is missing, and after a childhood of emotional neglect, it is unlikely the relationship with the mother will change. Perhaps you have experienced this feeling of never being satisfied and asking for more and more expressions of love from your partner. You may frequently ask for reassurance of love, "Do you *really* love me?" Regardless of the feelings your partner expresses to you, you never feel entirely loved. Again, you may begin to believe there is something wrong with you, and this leads to uncertainty in your thinking and feeling. "He says he loves me, but if he does, why do I continue to have this empty, fearful feeling?"

Like some women, you may have had healthy non-abusive partners in the past but found them unsatisfying. Healthy relationships won't last because a hungry woman's need for love and reassurance is never satisfied, so she either seeks "real love" elsewhere or her partner tires of the constant demand. No healthy person can withstand the pleading need of the unloved and lonely child/woman. Healthy men know it's a bottomless well. *The truth is the love you seek can never be found in an adult romantic relationship because that is not the type of love that is missing.* What's missing is the essential, unremitting love of a parent, most often the mother, which was never given and cannot be replaced.

Unfortunately, the only men who engage in emotionally needy relationships are insecure, controlling, and abusive. Both the needy woman and the abusive man are attracted to one another for all the wrong reasons, and they can find each other even in the dark. That is why the scenario of abusive relationships is repeated and will continue to be repeated until women discover that the kind of love they are seeking cannot be found in a romantic relationship. It must be met by a primary source and if that is impossible, which is most likely, there is only one person left—one's self.

Carl Jung wrote, "Hunger makes food into gods" (Campbell 1971, 42). As I described earlier, chocolate becomes magical after a life of oatmeal. The hunger for love makes the person who supplies it a god. And skin hunger makes the person who satisfies it a god, too. Attention, jealousy, sex—anything that fills the emptiness and keeps the Saber-Toothed Tiger at bay deserves worship. The fear of the Saber-Toothed Tiger is overwhelming and the hungry woman will do anything, endure any abuse, any torture, to avoid being devoured by the tiger. It explains why she can't leave. The cave opening is barred by the menacing presence of death in a most horrifying sense—acknowledgment that she was not wanted and could have been left to die. You face the reality that your life has always, from the moment of birth, been tenuous, not in the common sense that all life is, but because there was no one there who passionately cared if you lived or died.

One of the conditions for a diagnosis of Post Traumatic Stress Disorder is that one has "experienced, witnessed, or was confronted with an event or events that involved actual or threatened death ... or a threat to the physical integrity of self ..." (Diagnostic and Statistical Manual, IV-TR 2000, 467). If a child is aware, on whatever level, that her "being" is threatened from birth, she constantly experiences stress. The Saber-Toothed Tiger never leaves. As an adult she needs a constant, intense experience of affection and emotion and is thereby attracted to abusive men. The emotion has to be intense or it feels too close to the nothingness and the threat of loss of life repeatedly experienced in childhood. Unfortunately, this intense feeling is misinterpreted as love, but it is not. It is a "fix" for feeling emotionally destitute. For abused women, leaving an abuser does not mean returning to a former unmarried, single life. It means *losing* life, dying, a great emptiness, no longer being visible, not being, obliteration.

13

Flat-Headed Children

Abused women have children for all the wrong reasons. That's not so different from many people, but the conditions under which children of abused women are raised are unique and have more severe outcomes. Abused women see children as a captive source of unconditional love. You may recognize this in yourself. Your children were born, not to be loved for who *they* are, but to provide love and security to you. You are probably a good mother who loves your children passionately, and you show them you love them in many ways. You try to give them all the love you never had. In return, you believe they will *have* to love you! As I mentioned earlier, you're giving your children what *you* need. If you grew up in an affectionless, sterile family, you ensure your children will never go to bed without being told they are loved. You tell them daily and do all you can to show them how much they are loved. The same intensity of affection and indulgence shown to your abusing man is at times demonstrated with your children. You try to teach the abuser and the children how to love like you love. It has to be the most intense feeling or it doesn't feel like love— it feels like oatmeal and there is never enough. However, the constant cloying affection, even though well-intentioned, can result in the opposite of what you want. There is a strong message behind the emotion and it tells the children they must love you equally and as strongly in return. Children should not be the caretakers of their mother's emotional needs, and your constant demand for love blinds you to the real needs of your children. From birth, your children received the message that they *must* love and they must love in a way that attempts to meet an adult's need. They sense they are obligated to feed an insatiable hunger they don't understand. All this emotional leaning on children results in what I call "little flat-headed children." Their little heads become flattened on top from being leaned on by their needy mothers. The unwanted little girl in a woman's body doesn't live for her children. Her children live for her. Imagine the burden!

Mother's Little Man

Your need and demand for love has differing effects on boys and girls, and the effect on young boys differs depending on whether the abuser stays in the relationship or leaves. If the abusive relationship has ended, your son may become vulnerable to the expectation of taking the place of the adult male in the household. Unfortunately, after witnessing abuse, he may begin to take on the characteristics of the abuser, at times even telling you something like, "I'm in charge now." Because you need your son's love even more now that your abuser is gone, beware of giving that authority to your son. Boys, particularly if they have witnessed their fathers abusing their mothers, rebel in the way they've been taught—they become abusive to their mothers and/or siblings. I've witnessed how easy it is for a young boy to begin abusing his mother and sisters in the same way the abuser did. I have observed this behavior in boys as young as three and four years old. From my experience, if a boy reaches the age of eight before the mother leaves the abusive relationship, it is too late. The boy has learned the lesson well. His job is to control through force. He's tired of being leaned on, and in order to break away from Mom, he has to become like his role-model father. His other option is to continue to be his mother's emotional support, her "little man" in every sense of the word, and to push any resentment about his situation deep down inside. Chances are the young man with repressed resentment will either become depressed or eventually manage his feelings through drug or alcohol use.

A Son's Anger

If your son attempts to take on the heavy burden of fulfilling your need for love, he may again develop resentment. Because he's being emotionally leaned on, he may not be able to leave you to pursue healthy adult relationships. Now his resentment might turn to anger. A little boy who is required to fulfill the emotional needs of his mother grows up to perceive women as suffocating and emotionally demanding, and any inkling of demand becomes too much for him to bear. Since the boy is not allowed to "not love" his mother, his anger is displaced to some future girlfriend or wife, quite possibly resulting in physical abuse. He has been asked to undertake an impossible task and he knows it. While your son is young, he will not be able to articulate his resentment and anger because he simply does not have the understanding or vocabulary. Regardless of your son's age, eight or eighteen, it is not his job to replace your partner. As he matures, and if he becomes resentful and angry, he cannot express these feelings without also experiencing guilt. Certainly he will be confused about his anger toward a mother who repeatedly tells him how much he is loved. And you do love, but your love is like a heavy weight on his shoulders!

Double-Bind

If the abusive father remains in the relationship, the boy is placed in a terrible position. His mother expects him to protect her from the abuse, yet she also expects him to replace his father and fulfill her emotional needs. He literally has to choose between his mother and his own manhood and masculinity. If he chooses masculinity, he becomes like his role-model father and lives with ongoing guilt about betraying his mother. If he chooses his mother, the young man ends up in brief relationships and may even have children, but he will never fully commit to his partner because mom is always waiting in the wings, ready for her entrance onto the stage. She continues to play her role of lonely, needy woman and her son's guilt makes him answer her call for someone to lean on. He grows up to be a flat-headed man battling the Saber-Toothed Tiger for mom.

Mothers and Daughters

There are also several possible outcomes for daughters raised by abused mothers. After years of being emotionally leaned on, a daughter may also become resentful and contemptuous. She may begin acting out in an attempt to get her mother to attend to her actual needs. When this fails, she may engage in a relationship, either live-in or marriage, in order to leave home and be able to breathe. It is time for her own emotional needs to be addressed.

Another outcome is that daughter never completely disconnects, and although she may marry and have a family, she continues to feel responsible for her mother's emotional well-being. This type of mother-daughter relationship is one in which I hear mothers and daughters describe themselves as "best friends." Usually they arrive in my office together, sit very close on the sofa, and some have actually held hands throughout the session. They say they are together to "support" one another. The word "enmeshed" only partially describes this dynamic. Despite the "friends" façade, there is typically a pile of anger underneath.

Like the sons, daughters feel guilty too. When a daughter sacrifices her life for her mother's sake, she is going to feel angry and resentful. She will find these feelings incongruent with the thought that she is caring for her mother, ostensibly in return for all that supposed love her mother was giving to her. I always tell these "couples" that mothers are not supposed to be a daughter's friend. Mothers are to be parents! Often, in these cases, the daughters are unable to have a fulfilling relationship with a partner because they feel guilty if their first allegiance and responsibility is not to their mothers. They are pulled between caring for their mothers' emotional needs and trying to care for their own husbands and children. Sometimes they spend too much of their time rescuing their mothers from the next abusive relationship.

Grandmother, Daughter, Grandchildren

Abused women also make terrible grandmothers. They continue to need impossible love, and now that their own daughter's time is scattered between mother, husband, and children, grandma can just bypass her daughter and go straight to the little ones. So she starts lavishing gifts, affection, and time on her grandchildren. Her daughter thinks, *Why didn't you do that for me? You were so involved with your abusive man and you leaned on me. My head is flat and I'm tired and now you don't even think of returning all the energy I gave you because I was taught that I owed it to you! I'm really angry and sad.* Actually, daughters don't have these thoughts. They just have the feelings, and they don't make sense. After all, their mothers love them, right? They say so every blessed day! So why doesn't if feel like love?

The Next Generation

Your intense emotional need requires that a lot of time and attention be given to your abuser. It is as if you can see no one else. Abusers are demanding and attention has to be paid to every mood, every change of expression, and every whim, or violence might ensue. Abusers, by their nature, are often jealous of their own children and the time mothers spend with them. The abuser has to be first. Additionally, you may spend an inordinate amount of time pursuing your

The Saber-Toothed Tiger

own emotional security. Most of your family's time is spent on interaction between abuser and abused, leaving little time for your children and their emotional needs. I believe this is the true reason that daughters of abused women become involved in abusive relationships themselves. Not because they saw their mothers being abused and "learned" that behavior, but because their mothers did not have the time or emotional energy to spend on them when they were babies. The message of "not enough time" is repeated with the next generation, and children are again faced with the threat of a tenuous life and the stress that accompanies that reality. Remember that in addition to the "not enough time" message, the children of emotionally needy women were brought into the world not to be loved, but to give love, resulting in several threatening messages—"You *have* to love me but I'm too emotionally preoccupied to adequately meet your needs—your life depends on how you meet *my* needs." Thus the cycle of abuse continues into the next generation— another little girl who feels lonely and invisible. What appears to be a mother's love is really a mother's need and the Saber-Toothed Tiger continues to rule the cave.

Not all females raised in abusive homes end up in abusive relationships. The outcome depends on each individual situation, message, interpretation, intelligence, awareness, and other sources of love and affection. One child may not feel that her life is threatened because she was less aware, or had a loving babysitter, aunt, or grandparent. Birth order is also important. As I mentioned in chapter nine, Janet was the fourth female child. The firstborn did not experience the same lack of welcome into the family. She felt special and welcome. Every situation is different, and if you have been in an abusive relationship, it's likely you heard the same message as other women in the same position.

There is another scenario that I have observed when children refuse to cooperate in the leaning love. Some children simply are not mentally able to grasp the fact that they are being asked to give unconditional love. Others get the message early and get angry early, and some are so spoiled they can't conceive of having to give something back to their mothers. All the latter know is they are being continually asked for something they have no interest in giving. They too get angry and resentful—same outcome. Under these circumstances, if the abuser remains in the relationship, the need to keep him there is incredibly strong. Unable to obtain unconditional love from your children, you need your abuser more than ever. He can't ever withdraw his love. You can't be lonely or the tiger wins and you die. You are stuck. You can't leave. You can't allow your man to leave. You will do anything to keep your abuser. Your children, in one way or another, are the sacrificial lambs to keep the Saber-Toothed Tiger far away.

Children are not always sacrificed whole. At first they may be asked to give up something small—like the reality of their own thinking. They're told, "No, your father isn't a bad man. He loves us. He's just having a hard time at work. He didn't mean to hit Mommy." Eventually they are made to sacrifice their feelings, "You have to love your father. After all, he's your father. You don't know how lucky you are. I never had a father." At some point, they may have to sacrifice their safety, "If you hadn't opened your mouth, he wouldn't have hit you. You know he can't help it, just like when he hits me. Just stay out of it." In extreme cases some children are forced to sacrifice their bodies. The woman who sells her children, allows them to be sexually abused, or abuses them herself in order to placate her partner sacrifices her children for her own need to avoid loneliness.

Even if the children are spared physical or sexual abuse, they still sacrifice. One young woman I worked with named Wanita came from a middle class home where there were no incidences of physical abuse. Her parents remain happily married today. Yet Wanita became involved with a terribly abusive man while she was a teenager. We explored the events of her birth, her relationships with her siblings, and her interpretation of her life. Again her history revealed the same underlying need for affection and love. She was the firstborn in her family and shortly after birth it was discovered she had a severe medical problem. There was a realistic possibility that she might die, but her parents were not able to afford the medical care she needed. Wanita required an operation, but it had to be delayed for several years until enough money could be saved. During the wait, a second "healthy" daughter, Ashela, was born. Ashela had a possessive disposition and wanted their mother's attention most of the time. No one could fault Wanita's mother for enjoying her healthy baby. She was grateful she did not have to spend all of her time being a nurse to Ashela as she did with Wanita.

Wanita was two years old and felt rejected by her sister and mother. Her father worked two jobs in order to earn the money for her medical care and had little time to share with Wanita. On some level, Wanita knew there was something about her that created an inconvenience or problem. She was intelligent and highly sensitive, a trait that frequently accompanies high intellect. In time, Wanita received the medical help she needed, but the combination of feeling left out and apart from her mother and sister and the infrequent interaction with her father caused her to feel empty and lonely. Her existence had been threatened not only physically, but emotionally, and she grew up hungry and attracted to abusive men who could provide the emotional intensity she craved. Wanita's mother certainly did not intend to hurt her daughter. As a young mother it must have been very difficult to have a child that might not live. Maybe she blamed herself for Wanita's health problem, or could not allow herself to be close to a child who might die. It would be too painful to bear. I believe most mothers do the best they can with the skills and knowledge they have. It is so unfortunate that when a mother cannot love and welcome a baby into the world, the consequences are terrible and cumulative. Interestingly, when Ashela grew up, she did not become involved in abusive relationships, and she continues to have a close relationship with her mother.

As this story demonstrates, not all children are sacrificed, but some become sacrificial lambs. Their thinking, feelings, security, emotional stability, happiness, and, in actuality, their childhoods are sacrificed—intentionally or unintentionally—due to events and circumstances. To be loved is all that matters. The hunger must continually be fed.

Telling Children the Truth

When you decide to change from being a mother who creates flat-headed children, a difficult assignment is learning to tell your children the truth. If you have left your abuser and your children ask if Daddy will be coming home, tell the truth. You may be afraid that your children will be hurt if you tell them he will not be back, but they deserve honesty. Children ask about their fathers (stepfathers or surrogate fathers) for many different reasons. Sometimes they honestly miss them; after all, these men may have been significant in the children's lives. Other times, they are asking for assurance that they don't have to be afraid of the abuser anymore. They may also be asking what they should expect in the future. Their lives have been disrupted and they are uncertain about what has happened. It is important to find out what the child is really asking and answer honestly, without hostility or negative comments about the abuser. Avoid comments such as, "No, the bastard is never coming back! Don't you remember how awful he was to me? It sounds like you care more about him than you do your own mother!" Children do not need to hear more hurtful words. They need to believe you are in control and able to take care of them. A healthy response to their question is, "No, Daddy isn't going to come home, but I'm here and I'll take care of you. I love you and you will be okay." Of course, older children are going to have a deeper understanding of what has happened, and information given to children should be appropriate for their age and experience. It is very important that you not use this opportunity to again lean on the child for emotional support. An attitude of strength and self-sufficiency should be conveyed. The children need to know they will be cared for and that their lives are secure.

Children become resentful at giving up their own emotional needs in order to satisfy their mother's longing. The mother's effort to get unconditional love from her children fails because the children realize *their* needs are not important and they rebel. Unconditional love doesn't develop. The children are smothered and gasping for air. A responsible mother stands on her own two feet and doesn't raise flat-headed children.

14

Learning to Love Yourself

So here you are—a hollow woman, physically and/or emotionally threatened, feeling unwanted and unloved from birth, with a hunger and fear so great you will endure any amount of abuse, even death, to avoid the Saber-Toothed Tiger of loneliness. A disposable human being. How do you become healthy, leaving both the oatmeal and the chocolate behind? It *is* possible, for as I've worked with women over the years I've seen many successes. There have also been many times when the fear of the Saber-Toothed Tiger is too great and women return to their abusers and the abuse increases. I have discovered that when an abused woman engages in counseling with me and stays until all aspects of therapy are completed, she is able to end the abusive relationship, and she avoids getting involved with another abuser. I am so convinced that my concept is correct because I've counseled women who had repeated abusive relationships, but following our counseling, they were able to recognize abusers and were no longer attracted to the men who offered the sugar rush. And abusive men were no longer attracted to them. Abusers aren't attracted to healthy women.

There is the mistaken idea among abused women that if one simply does not become involved in a relationship for a very long time following abuse, the next relationship will be different. I counseled a woman who left her first abusive relationship and avoided any long-term involvements for the next eighteen years. She waited until her son left home for college before even considering another relationship. She thought if she obtained self-sufficiency and maturity she would never end up in another abusive relationship. Wrong. During all those years of earning financial self-sufficiency, she never discovered why she initially selected an abusive man. She thought it "just happened." It was him—he was at fault. And certainly he was. There is no excuse for his behavior. But it was also her. She picked him for the chocolate, the end of oatmeal, to become visible, but only in his eyes. She still carried the emotional hunger from childhood and the very first meaningful relationship after eighteen years became abusive shortly after the wedding. When she came to counseling, it was time to really find out what was going on and begin working on her self.

Accepting Reality

The first step in healing is to accept reality and no longer deny what you have known all along—your parents did not love you *the way that you needed to be loved*. I say *the way you needed to be loved* because most parents believe they love their children. However, as discussed in the Still-Face studies, an infant responds with distress when there is parental disinterest, little eye contact, avoidance of interaction, minimal physical contact, and when there is only enough care to physically survive but not emotionally thrive. I recall a session with one woman who had described a bland, emotionally barren childhood. When we arrived at this point in therapy, she cried, "I don't know if I could live knowing my mother didn't love me!" What she meant was she didn't think she could live after admitting the truth. She had already lived a life without her mother's love.

This part of treatment, the acknowledgment of one's emotional childhood, is crucial, and you may experience a terrible feeling of loss. Allow yourself to cry for what should and could have been. Allow yourself to cry a child's tears for want of a mother's love. Allow yourself to grieve the death of hope for your mother's constant and unconditional love. Give up the hope that, "If I try hard enough, I will be loved." Grief is not simply a confirmation that the sadness and loneliness you felt as a child was real and predictable. Instead, it is the beginning of growth and an acknowledgment of what you unconsciously believed about yourself through your entire life—that you are a survivor, you willed *yourself* to live. As a child, everyday you outwitted the Saber-Toothed Tiger and survived. Somewhere deep inside, you held onto hope and never gave up on yourself. Now the work of becoming visible begins, and the first step is to become visible to yourself. Know this—just because you were unimportant to your parents does not mean you are unimportant. If your parents didn't love you, then who is left? If you have children, you will most likely reply, with a sense of satisfaction, "My kids will love me. I have my kids." I remind you that it is not a child's responsibility to provide love to a parent, but the other way around. Parental love is displayed by being a responsible parent, not by being your children's best friend. A responsible parent is stable—emotionally, financially, morally, and intellectually. A responsible parent provides for and teaches her children. If you are like most abused women, you are a loving but lenient parent. The hunger doesn't allow for much discipline, because the kids might get angry and not "like" you, and it is they who make you feel loved. So you bend and bend and try to please them and care for them—you take it to the extreme. "If I just show them how much I love them, they'll love me back the same way and I'll finally be loved the way I need to be loved." As we've learned, an abused woman spends her children's lives giving them what she herself needs, and it is always an overbearing, cloying emotion. Children know when they are loved—okay, enough of it! They need other things too, such as a sense of individuality and independence.

Self-Love

So now that we've determined that you were not wanted and loved the way you needed to be as an infant or child and you cannot use your children to fill that need, who's left? Just you. It is entirely up to you to fill the emptiness you've carried for so long. Let's begin by getting a sheet of paper and pen, and at the top of the paper write the title, "All the Ways I Love Myself." Now begin listing all the evidence that shows that you love yourself. If you are like most women I see, you will have difficulty with this task. For many, the assignment is very challenging and some women are unable to report even one example of self-love. Like them, you are probably so accustomed to showing everyone else how much you love them that you've forgotten to love yourself. Your life has been about caring for everyone else in the hope that someone would love you in return. Unfortunately, this type of behavior does not result in what you desire. Instead, you end up being taken advantage of by both your abuser and your children, and you continue to feel lonely, unloved, and quite possibly angry and resentful. You certainly won't receive the kind of love you want from unbalanced giving.

You might *say* you love yourself, but we aren't looking for words here. Just as I asked you to give proof of parental love, again you must provide hard evidence; in other words, observable behaviors that clearly show self-love. Little things such as manicures, styling your hair, dressing nicely, buying yourself a piece of jewelry, and taking time for a long bath, can be examples of self-love. Now, you may well have done these things while you were in your relationship. In fact, you most likely paid too much attention to how you looked. The difference here is that instead of treating yourself well because you loved yourself, you did these things in order to meet the expectations, and sometimes the demands, of your abuser. You probably were expected to be perfect and fulfill his idealized image of a wife or girlfriend. Therefore, it is important to stress that these acts of self-love must have been undertaken for you alone, and you must determine which ones were self-satisfying. It is now time to focus on your own needs and wants. If you are having a hard time completing the list of ways you love yourself, you might begin another list of things you enjoy (and it can not include taking care of others!). This will help you realize what you have left out of your life and give you a starting place to begin taking care of you. After you have made your list, you have to begin applying self-love every day. Each day you must behave in ways that demonstrate you love yourself. At first, in order to keep yourself focused and honest, you may want to write down what you do each day that shows how you love yourself.

The Importance of "No"

Along with the need to care-take in exchange for love, you probably rarely say no, particularly to the people you love. (Although we will talk about it here, you will learn *how* to say no in chapter eighteen.) I have heard untold numbers of stories of women who kept trying to manage credit card payments after their husbands or boyfriends overspent on "toys" for themselves. Some women even bought expensive gifts for their abusers, yet their children went without basic needs. In abusive relationships there is an incredible focus on what the abuser wants, because the tranquility of the home depends on his happiness, and abused women take on the job of ensuring that his every desire is fulfilled.

The inability to say no, along with the guilt created when the man's wants are put before the children's and the fear of not being loved, all feed into the lack of discipline within an abusive home. Additionally, if the father doesn't have to limit himself in any way, why should the children? Again, the male children learn early how important men's wants are and the females learn it is their job to care for the males. The girls become very resentful about males always coming first and grow up to distrust and dislike men. They may have boyfriends and eventually husbands, but they may continue to have underlying hostility toward men. They may select passive men and take on the role of abuser, belittling and emotionally abusing their partners.

The most important reason for not saying no in an abusive relationship is that it leads to violence. Perhaps not immediately, but "the man as the victim" believes he *deserves* what he wants and if he doesn't get it, he eventually gets angry or resentful and becomes violent. Therefore, saying no is dangerous. Learning to say no will be an important component in loving yourself.

15

The Hitler Voice

Now that you've gained awareness of how your emotional history has influenced your choice of a partner, and you're beginning to give yourself the love and attention you once gave to others, it is time to recognize and talk back to the "Hitler Voice." I have to give credit to one of the women in group for the name. She was physically and sexually abused by a male relative well into her teen years. Eventually, she was able to escape his control, and she moved several thousand miles away to our local women's shelter in order to gain her freedom and be far enough away to feel safe. She provided the perfect name for the voice that resides in your head long after you have left your abuser.

The phenomenon commonly known as "brainwashing" occurs subtly in abusive relationships. At first, it may be just a comment of displeasure or dislike. Remember Janet? From the very beginning she wanted to please Darren and was willing to change whatever was needed.

"Before I married Darren, I bought myself wonderful clothes. I liked to look professional and shopped at the nicest stores. I had shoes and jewelry, handbags; you name it, I had it. I loved dressing up! You know, when I was growing up my family didn't have much money, and with all those older sisters I got a lot of hand-me-downs. I studied the fashion magazines and I would copy the makeup and hairstyles and I tried to find clothes like the ones that were up-to-date. I got a lot of compliments too!"

The Saber-Toothed Tiger

Janet laughed while she recalled those happier times, but her demeanor changed and she frowned as she related how Darren saw her.

"It took several trips for me to move all my clothes—those clothes I was so proud of. Darren started right in saying I had 'old-woman clothes.' He asked if I had anything with some color. I was hurt and told him those were my work clothes. You know, I think now he was jealous because I had a good job. He just kept on saying he knew what men liked. And I just went along. In my house men always knew better than women."

Recall that during her childhood, Janet observed men being treated more importantly than women. When Darren criticized Janet's taste and clothing, she reacted in a way that could be expected. She had learned that men know better than women. The voices from her childhood culture and community remained in her head, and Janet's self-confidence shrank just a little. Janet desperately wanted Darren's approval and love. It would be a small thing to make him happy by dressing like he wanted. Over the years, her entire wardrobe was replaced by clothes that Darren had picked out. Nowhere was there a trace of Janet's former look.

I've heard that same story a hundred times. The criticism applies to just about every aspect of a woman's life and it derives from her partner's feelings of either inadequacy or arrogance. Sometimes, the latest message is incongruent with an earlier message. For example, one time your partner may compliment you on your makeup and hair, so the next day you try to please him and keep his attention by looking the same way. But this time he reacts with disdain, "What's with the slutty look? You have a boyfriend or something?" Abusers use whatever works to keep you off-guard, unsure, and feeling inadequate. Whatever mood he is in, whatever he wants at the moment, must be met—change your hair, change your make-up, change your clothes, change how you talk, change how you think, change how you are, change who you are. Eventually, you are whatever he wants you to be, whenever he wants it. You no longer know what *you* like, what *you* think, or who *you* are. You must be the ideal; the perfect female. His voice lives in your brain. Anything for love—feed the hunger.

When you leave your abuser, the Hitler Voice doesn't automatically become silent. In fact, you may be so accustomed to it that you don't recognize it as foreign. You became the plastic blow-up doll with few thoughts of your own, and any thoughts you did have, you filtered through your abuser's point of view, checking twice to make sure you weren't putting your life, and more importantly, your love, in danger. Remember, there was incredible fear behind your behavior. Fear of violence, not being loved, but mostly fear of the Saber-Toothed Tiger—loneliness. In your mind both physical harm and loneliness can result in death. Therefore, you listened and responded to the voice that told you how to be. It is well ingrained in your mind. It's a scary thought that someone else's voice lives in your head, but it's true, and it takes awareness and talking back to make it go away.

The No Contact Rule

An important part of leaving your abuser is the "no contact" rule. Any communication with your abuser is dangerous, both physically and emotionally. Contact will take you right back into the emotionality of the relationship. You can easily see how verbal contact would have a strong influence on your thinking and behavior. After all, you're well practiced at listening and responding to his wishes and commands. If you have contact with him, he will play either the victim or the commander. When he is the victim he will tell you how he can't live without you. He may even threaten to kill himself. He'll cry and apologize and although you've heard it before, hope will make you believe and you'll go back to him again.

Remember, nothing will change, but it will reinforce the fact that he can do anything to you and you will never leave. The abuse will worsen.

If you're in a safe place and you have the courage to tell your abuser you aren't going back, and you tell him firmly, he will immediately stop being the victim and become the commander. The anger, the name-calling (whore, slut, bitch), the accusations of infidelity, the put-downs ("Nobody's going to want you—look at you!"), the threats (he'll tell you exactly how he's going to harm or kill you or your family) will all start. You know the drill. If being pitiful doesn't work, he'll threaten. You will again be afraid.

You can see how contact will affect you. You end up afraid. More of the same feeling you're trying to get rid of by leaving him. I recommend you change your telephone number, and if that isn't feasible, monitor your calls. If you see his number, do not answer. If he repeatedly calls, turn off the phone. If he calls from an unfamiliar number and you answer, hang up as soon as you hear his voice. E-mail is a no-brainer—delete without reading them. Or, if you have a restraining order against him, save the e-mails and take them to the police as evidence that he is harassing you. I have a different rule for postal mail, however. You may indeed open the card or letter to look for money or checks, and if found, keep the cash or cash the check and then burn the correspondence without reading it or turn it over to your attorney or the police. *No cheating!* Everyone laughs at the last rule. Fat chance there's going to be any money.

I also advise you not to have contact through friends or relatives. They will tell you how sad he is, and you will want to rescue him. After all, it used to be your job to make him happy. The most hurtful thing you will hear is that he has found a new girlfriend. You will feel hurt and angry. You will also ruminate about why he couldn't love you like he loves her. You'll fall into the trap of wondering what's wrong with you and where you failed. Haven't you had enough of that kind of thinking? Remember, that's the Hitler Voice trying to control you. When others start telling you about him, put your hand up and firmly say, "Stop! I don't want to hear it." If they continue, you say it again and again, or walk away.

The "no contact" rule is the most important change you will have to make during the initial period of healing. It allows time away from the Hitler Voice and gives you the opportunity to listen to your own voice. This takes time, and you will need to confront and question whose voice you are hearing. If you begin to question the importance of your dreams, hear a voice telling you how selfish you are, or are thinking in any of the negative ways your abuser would like you to think, stop and talk back. If necessary, say it out loud. Tell the voice and yourself you will no longer allow yourself to be controlled or manipulated. Tell the voice, yourself, and the world how important you are and how you will be loved and treated well. Say it again and again and make it true. Prove to yourself your own importance, your own self-love. Go back to your lists of things you enjoy and ways you show yourself love and *act* on them. Remember you have to *do*, not just *say*. In time, you will be able to distinguish your voice from your abuser's, and eventually the Hitler Voice will fade away and vanish.

Taking Back What's Yours

If you have left your abuser, you may, like many other women in your situation, purposely avoid going to places or doing things you actually like because you are reminded of him. Staying away from painful reminders may be beneficial at first, but eventually you need to return to doing the things you like regardless of the feelings they evoke. It is the same as standing up to your abuser again. One woman related that after leaving her abuser, she avoided eating a special bakery treat because it was something they had shared during good times. Together they would walk to a neighborhood bakery and share a scrumptious éclair. When she passed the bakery, warm but painful memories returned, and she relived her lost dream. Nevertheless, she was determined not to allow her abuser to permanently take away this small pleasure. She returned to the bakery, bought an éclair, took it home and hid in the bathroom so her children wouldn't see her. With tears streaming down her face she ate the dessert and took one more step toward owning her life. It takes strength and determination to stop your abuser's Hitler Voice and his continued control of your thoughts and your life. Before you return to a special place or event, be aware of how you might feel and then go anyway. The more you associate the place or action with your new freedom and enjoyment, the less it will remain chained to the past. In this way you take back another piece of your life and give it new meaning.

When There Has to be Contact

Realistically, there are times when contact does have to take place, such as exchanging children for visitation if the court ordered it. I encourage you to make the exchange in front of a police station or in a public place—never at your home. Any verbal interaction should be kept to a minimum. For example, "I will meet you here at six PM on Sunday to pick up the kids." Any information about prescriptions, play dates, school programs, homework, etc. can be written and handed or faxed to him. If he tries to engage you in conversation, do not reply. If he is not rewarded in his efforts to engage you in conversation, he will eventually stop trying. Of course, all legal matters, such as divorce, property settlements, and child support issues should be communicated through attorneys. There's no need to discuss these issues with your abuser at all.

    No contact is an essential part of getting rid of the Hitler voice. A wound won't heal if you keep picking at it, and any contact is just that. Contact just makes the wound bleed more and there is a good chance it will become infected.

16

Sitting With The Tiger and Fear of Freedom

> Loneliness
> can be so real
> it can feel
> like sand
> in the palm
> of your
> hand.
>
> Maya Angelou Hallmark Collection 2001

Since your fear of being lonely is what kept you in abusive relationships, the only way out of the cave is to face the tiger. This is the most difficult but most essential step on your path to becoming healthy. You understand where your feelings of loneliness come from and you know that this frightful feeling will not kill you. Now it is time to re-experience loneliness. Many women make ongoing excuses to avoid this part of the healing process, for indeed it is the scariest part, but I cannot emphasize more strongly how important this step is. If you don't sit with the tiger, you will never be entirely free.

After you've left your abuser, found a safe environment, grieved your losses, and begun to practice self-love, it is time to begin your relationship with the Saber-Toothed Tiger. The exercise itself is really quite simple. Find a place in your home where there is likely to be little distraction. You can sit on the floor or in a chair, but no beds or sofas—you have to sit, not lie down. No falling asleep in the middle of the exercise. Once

The Saber-Toothed Tiger

you have decided on your place to meet the tiger, you are to go there every day and spend as much time there alone as you can endure. You cannot read, watch television, listen to music, knit, whistle, sing, talk on the telephone, or do anything other than *sit*. You are to sit alone, without any distraction. Do not confuse this assignment with meditation. You are not going to meditate. Meditation puts you in a relaxed, detached brainwave state. Your goal is not to remove yourself from the everyday in order to avoid feeling. Your goal is to feel the most dreadful feeling, loneliness, the feeling you have been avoiding all your life. Be brave!

At first it may be hard to spend even five or ten minutes sitting with the Saber-Toothed Tiger, but eventually you should aim for at least an hour. (Yes, I know that finding an hour may be difficult, especially if you have young children, and you may have to plan your time with the tiger after the children are in bed. It doesn't matter if you are tired; getting healthy is hard work and it is yours to do.) As you sit alone, the Saber-Toothed Tiger will arrive and you will experience the loneliness you have tried so hard to deny. Allow yourself to feel whatever you feel—anxiety, fear, anger, but most importantly, loneliness. Allow any thoughts and memories to come forth. Again you may cry and grieve for yourself. Some people find it helpful to write their feelings and thoughts in a journal after their time with the tiger. I repeat: this exercise is the essence of your healing. Without it you will never be free of your past.

Each day you should strive to increase the time you spend alone with the tiger. As you do this work, the loneliness will slowly begin to transform. The longer you allow yourself to experience the feeling, the less frightening it will be. Over time, you will adapt to loneliness and this horrible, scary feeling will become just another emotion. It will never become pleasant, but it will be bearable. This is how you earn your freedom.

Josée Perrine

Fear of Freedom

Fear of freedom sounds like an odd idea. After being controlled and abused, one would think freedom would be delicious. Usually, it is about as frightening as the Saber-Toothed Tiger. I say "about" because it doesn't feel exactly the same. Initially, freedom is equated with loneliness. After a lifetime of self-enforced bondage to another human being, it is frightening to disconnect and stand alone. However, once you understand why loneliness is so scary, freedom becomes distinct. Freedom is the unknown. It also means there is no one to lean on and no one to blame. And freedom comes with a handy sidekick—responsibility. It means, yes, you are now free to no longer be bruised or broken, free to hold your head up, free to dress the way you like, free to have your own friends, free to cut your hair if you want, free to stay out as long as you like, free to have a job, free to pay your own bills, free to live in a smaller house or apartment, free to apply for food stamps, free to go to the free clinic for your children's medicines, free to worry about the quality of day care your children are receiving, free to worry about going to court to extend the temporary restraining order against your abuser, free to worry whether he will kidnap the kids in order to get even with you for leaving him, free to feel tired and guilty after working a ten-hour shift because you don't want to be the mother tonight, free to have sex by yourself, free to ache for another person, free to eat toast because you are too tired to cook anything. You get the picture. Freedom comes with a cost and that cost can be one more reason why you think of returning to your abuser. It is very hard work to be free, especially if you have a couple of children and not much money.

You fought fiercely to gain your freedom and to stand up to your abuser. You may have thought that was the end of it, but it proved to be the beginning of something else. You may want to spend some time on the pity-pot, but that would diminish your courage. Freedom is not cheap and responsibility can be a real pain in the ass. I tell women, "If you walk this path, you will be the strongest person you know." You may also be the bravest. It takes enormous courage to leave an abuser. It takes courage to face an unknown future, sometimes with negligible skills and resources. It takes courage to pick yourself up from the emotional blows of an empty childhood and try to fashion a future of love and self-reliance. We give medals, lovely purple hearts on ribbons, to men who have endured warfare. We reward their courage and bravery, and we should. What do we give the thousands of women who take the punches meant for their children? Women who go to work because they need the money, covering their bruises with makeup? How do we reward the good intentions of the woman who desperately believes she is responsible for keeping the family together, who tries to live up to her religious teachings? Abused women risk their lives every day for their children, their families, and most of all, for love. Where are their ribbons? You are now free to fashion your own reward.

Freedom is scary at first, but every step, every accomplishment leads to another. I have seen satisfaction and joy on the faces of women who found jobs that paid seven dollars an hour and were accepted into low-income housing because it meant they were free and no longer had to depend on an abusive man. I have also seen the same women earn better jobs and homes, and the pride they have in themselves is worth more to them than any mansion. They know the value of their freedom. Fear is just a feeling. You must do what you need to do regardless of how you feel. As you move toward your goals, the fear will fade and be replaced with pride and ownership of your life.

This may sound unbelievable, but it is even possible to reach a point of gratefulness for what you have experienced. Certainly, no one wants to relive it, but the freedom to be yourself and the knowledge you have gained is incredibly rewarding, and you would not have learned it without this particular life. Sure, life looks scary, but nothing like the fear of the Saber-Toothed Tiger. That fear may never entirely go away and that can be a good thing. It can be a little reminder that keeps you alert and aware of old behaviors, feelings, and needs. The Saber-Toothed Tiger is your best teacher—something to be thankful for after the lesson is learned and the upheaval of change is in the past. You have survived not only the attempts on your life by your abuser, but something more frightening—loneliness and the crushing fear of death that was imprinted on your psyche at birth. The achievement of survival is yours. Freedom—no one can ever hurt you again. No one and nothing will ever own you again. You have triumphed over the Saber-Toothed Tiger.

17

Future Tense

You've come a long way on your journey toward freedom, and your next task is to turn your attention ahead and design your future. Your life probably became so wrapped around your abuser that you've forgotten what your goals used to be. Or maybe you were too young to have set goals. In order to begin planning a future, you might have to return to a more distant past. When you were a young woman, what were your dreams? What did you want to do with your life? What feeds your soul? What do you want to do, be, and have in your future?

The women I've written about were able to realize their dreams after they worked on repairing themselves. Janet went back to school and became a school teacher. Wanita obtained her master's degree and works with disabled children. Another woman found satisfaction doing clerical work for a social agency. Whatever you choose doesn't have to be grand as long as you are happy and living your own life. You might live what looks to others as a very ordinary life. Remember, your life, your survival, is more than ordinary. Your own happiness is all that matters.

You may not have the resources to pursue your dreams immediately, but keep the dreams alive for your future. Remember, you are allowed to change your mind as you go along. You are free to make your own life. Let's begin right now. You will need four sheets of notebook paper—or paper big enough to hold your thoughts and goals. On the first sheet, begin by writing down all the things you thought you wanted to do when you grew up. Don't be afraid of how silly they may seem now. Just be that kid again who dreamed. Did you want to be a ballerina, a doctor, teacher, or writer? If you had no particular dream, what did you do that you felt really good about? Did you work on your school's yearbook? Were you exceptional at sports? Did you have fun creating your own fashions? Did you like to work outside? Don't dismiss anything you loved as unimportant. Everything has some value in helping you find your future.

After completing the first list, start a second list of all the things you've done so far—jobs, volunteer work, and household chores. While you are writing this list, think about the skills that are needed to do these things. Not just the obvious or required skills, but the attendant knowledge and abilities—organization, time management, friendliness, empathy, and so on. If you are unsure or unaware of your skills, ask people who know you what they think you are good at. You might be surprised at what others have found valuable and helpful about you.

The third list will consist of the opportunities realistically available to you now. List what you will need in order to pursue the possible goals you have identified. Also list where you can go to get help. Are you eligible for grants for college? Do you need to earn your General Education Diploma? Can you get training through your state's vocational rehabilitation? Is a small business loan available to you? If you don't know what is available in your community, call the social services agency for your area. Many cities have a family resource center that can direct you to particular agencies that provide specific programs or assistance. And of course, if your town has a women's shelter, that will be a wonderful resource for referrals.

Now, after reviewing your three lists, select three goals that you think are realistic given your skills, time, location, and resources. Investigate how you can pursue these dreams.

Spend some time exploring the possibilities. Then make a decision, remember to ignore the Hitler Voice if it interferes, and consult your intuition as well as your intellect. Then begin!

There's one more point to be made here. You are not too old! I never let anyone off the hook of responsibility for claiming they are too old to begin something new. In ten or twenty years you will be ten or twenty years older regardless of what you chose to do with your life now. You might as well fill the time with something rewarding and worthwhile. No ageism allowed. I will, however, address the issue of disability, since occasionally my groups have members who are disabled. First understand that disabled doesn't mean "not able to do anything." Your time, talent, caring, and knowledge has value. You can always volunteer. Find what feeds your soul and contact an agency, church, library, or senior citizen's center and give to others. You have value. How you manage your disability can provide inspiration to others. Your example can teach someone else the virtues of acceptance and self love. It is time to give back.

Again, once you decide on a future direction, you are allowed to change your mind. If things aren't going in the direction you expected, return to your lists, update them, and start again. It's your journey; walk it, run it, ride it, fly it, just make sure you enjoy it.

18

Practice Dating and Being Healthy

If you are just recently out of an abusive relationship, or thinking of leaving one, this chapter is not yet for you. But if you have at least a year, or better yet, two years of freedom, no contact with your abuser, a finalized divorce, counseling, and future-oriented movement under your belt and you are interested in another relationship, this chapter will help you take the next step. The reason I recommend two years of independence before dating is because from my observations, that is the amount of time it usually takes to get free, especially if divorce with property and custody issues are involved. It also takes time to reorient your life and learn to be emotionally self-sufficient. It is not only time, however, that is important. It is what you do during that time, such as learning about yourself. Recall the woman I mentioned earlier who waited eighteen years, but didn't change anything about herself during that time, and selected another abuser for her next partner? It is imperative that you take enough time to work on you. This will be the hardest work you ever do, but the making of a fine product takes effort and time.

The very idea of dating may be scary. That's why you must practice before engaging in anything close to serious. Ideally, while you practice, you will be referring back to this book. This will help you stay safe and not return to former ways of thinking and behaving. You may want to seek professional counseling in order to get feedback about your thinking, feelings, and actions. However, the final decision about what you choose to do is always yours. That's what this whole process is about—listening to your own voice, trusting your thinking and feelings, and taking responsibility for your own freedom.

The goal of finding your way into the future is not to end up disliking and distrusting all men. Your future is yours, whether you chose to date, remarry, live with a partner, or give up on it all together is up to you—it is a choice. As you get healthy, you will no longer be interested in the men you used to need. You will be looking for the man who is independent, self-respecting, and as capable as you have become. But it takes some practice and you will need to be aware of the danger signs. Below are some of the signs of an abusive person that will help you evaluate the men you date:

- He is emotionally abusive, i.e., puts you down, insults you, or acts annoyed when you take the initiative to do things.
- He tries to control who you have as friends, how you dress, or how you choose to live your life.
- He talks derogatorily or tells demeaning jokes about the opposite sex.
- He is overly jealous.
- He abuses drugs and/or alcohol, or encourages you to use even if you do not want to.
- He pressures you to engage in sex although you may not want to.
- He is physically aggressive with you or others in order to get his way.
- He becomes overly angry when he experiences frustration.
- He thinks of women as being inferior and subservient, "less than."
- He becomes so angry that you change what you say or do in order to avoid his angry behavior.
  —Lauer, R. and Lauer, J. 2007

When you decide to go out with someone, don't be afraid to ask direct questions about his past and listen carefully to the answers. If he has had past relationships, how did they end and how does he talk about his past lovers? If he blames them for the break-up, calls them names, and/or appears still angry and resentful, don't linger. This person is angry at women and obviously holding a grudge. This type of behavior is another red flag. You don't want to be the person he takes his anger out on. Most importantly, if you feel even the least bit like you want to rescue him, if any of those old feelings of "I can show you what it is like to be really loved" start bubbling to the surface, get away quickly! If you don't, you are headed for your next abusive relationship. Remember, you are not looking for someone who *needs* you. You are looking for someone who likes, admires, and appreciates who you are, someone who *wants* to be with you, not someone who will lean on you or someone you can lean on. You are going to stand up straight from now on!

Protecting Yourself

I said to ask questions, but that doesn't mean you should sit him under a bare light bulb and fire away. Asking questions implies interest, and most people like it when others think they are interesting. One of the most effective ways to get information about a person is to say, "Tell me about your work/family/hobbies/kids/pets." Then listen to the story. Are there any gaps? Is there something that doesn't quite fit with what you know about him already? If he avoids discussing some topics, or appears annoyed that you ask about certain things, make a note of it. Follow up later if you chose to see him again. "Tell me about" certainly sounds direct, but this is the new you, the confident, capable you that is taking charge of her life. If this guy doesn't like you, it doesn't matter. You are over *needing* to be liked or loved. You love and respect yourself.

It seems logical that if you expect your date to be open and honest with you, you should be the same with him. However, this is not the case. Right now you have to be careful because you are practicing. Therefore, until you are well practiced and fully committed to a relationship, you need not disclose to anyone the abuse you have experienced. The reason for this is quite simple—until you can trust yourself and believe your partner to be trustworthy, you should not take the chance of opening that door for someone else to come in and hurt you, either physically or emotionally. Some abusers, who have not shown their abusiveness so far, will know how to manipulate you into returning to your former neediness. They will know how to tap into your need and you will be back where you started. Other people may be critical or try to analyze you, "You must be really dumb/insecure/have low self-esteem (fill in the blank)—if you stayed with him." You've probably heard all the usual comments in that regard. You don't need to hear any more of them and you've quit allowing people to beat you up in any manner, so don't share your history with anyone who is incapable of understanding it. You are not keeping your history a secret because you are ashamed. You are honoring yourself by not sharing it with those who will not respect your strength and your victory.

Setting Boundaries

By limiting what you share with others and not allowing people to enter your emotional space, you are setting boundaries. Think of your emotional space as a house. Let's pretend you live in a house and your house has a front door and a little porch. You have a nice fenced yard and a front walk from your porch to the gate. Outside the gate there is a sidewalk and then a public street. You don't (or at least you shouldn't) invite just anyone who happens to be passing by to enter your home. You invite into your home the people you know well and whose company you enjoy. Some people knock on the door and you open it. But maybe you are not interested in what they are selling, so you talk with them politely while they stand outside the door. Another time you might anticipate the pizza you ordered and meet the delivery person at the gate. Sometimes there are stray animals that you don't want in your yard so you make sure the gate is tightly closed. And sometimes there are people you don't even want on the public street! Your emotional space should be treated the same as your living space. You only invite into your home the people you trust to respect you and your home. Your abuser and those who treat you unkindly belong out on the street. Don't even let them in the yard! To put it more bluntly, you don't want all the neighborhood dogs crapping in your yard, and especially not in front of your door. Don't let anyone dump emotional crap on your doorstep either.

The emotional and physical boundaries you set for yourself are important, and you set them by telling people clearly what is not allowed and what you require from them in your space. For example, if a man begins to behave in a controlling or jealous manner toward you, you say, "I am not anyone's possession. Don't tell me how to act." An abusive person will most likely get angry and call you an obscene name. Good. You won't have to waste any more time to find out the truth about him. If you have happened upon a manipulative and cunning abuser, he may apologize. Don't be fooled. He's already shown his true colors. Never mistake control and jealousy as love. Remember, you've already learned that. It doesn't mean he really, really loves you. It means he's a controlling, jealous, abusive man. Sweep the crap off your doorstep!

In chapter fourteen I wrote that you would learn about saying no. An important aspect of setting boundaries is learning how to say no and stopping there. Most women I've counseled have become accustomed to providing lengthy explanations for their thoughts, behaviors, and feelings. They think they have to defend any decision or statement they make. If you have ever left your abuser and continued to have contact with him, you may have had an exchange that he started, and the dialogue went something like this:

"Let's talk about this break up. I want to come over and talk to you."

"No." This is where you should stop, but you've probably said something like the following. "I don't want to talk about it."

"Why not? We used to talk all the time. What's the matter with you?"

"There's nothing the matter with me. It's over and I don't want to talk about it." However, you're already talking about it!

"What, you're saying there's no chance? I don't understand you. You said you loved me, but now I know you were always lying. I can't trust you."

"I did love you, but you were mean to me, you hit me."

"You know I didn't mean it. You just get me so mad sometimes. I love you and I thought you loved me too."

"I did love you, but it just can't go on like this. I'm scared of you and I'm not responsible for you getting angry."

"Look, we love each other. I won't get angry any more. I promise...."

See how it goes? If you say anything more than *no*, you are indeed engaged in a conversation, and like every other talk you've had with your abuser, this exchange will end up exactly the same—you will be back in an abusive relationship and nothing will have changed. I promise.

One of the most difficult things you may have to learn is to say no, and then shut up, hang up, or walk away. You will need practice, so I recommend going to the grocery store—it doesn't have to be the one you regularly frequent, in case you feel uncomfortable with this exercise. Here's what you do: go to a grocery store, get your groceries, proceed to the checkout, and when the bagger asks, "Is plastic okay?" you say, "No, I want paper." (Or the opposite, of course, if he says paper.) After several trips to the grocery store and practicing "No, I want paper," then you begin replying by simply saying no. Let the bagger figure out that you want the opposite of whatever was suggested. Practice this at least three times a week for three weeks.

The second part of this exercise is for you to pay attention to your feelings following these interactions. Some women tell me they initially feel as if they have done something wrong or hurt someone's feelings, but afterwards they feel good about stating what they want. You might be pleasantly surprised at how free and in charge you feel. This exercise may sound silly, but I guarantee you, if you are a person who has difficulty saying no and that's all, this may be harder than you think. If you practice saying no in different situations at least three times a week, after a few weeks you will be looking for opportunities to say no simply because it feels so good.

Also, whereas a smile in this situation is entirely appropriate, for now you need to say what you want or don't want without a smile. The reason for this is that girls and women generally learn to behave incongruently when saying no. We learn early on that if we say no as if we mean it, we are told that we are not lady-like, or "who do you think you are?" or the most common retort, "what a bitch!" Girls learn young that to say no makes them a bad person.

Think about times in your own life when you have really not wanted to do something (like go out with someone or have sex) and you said everything but no. You said, "I don't think so," or "maybe later," or "let's do (fill in the blank) first," or "I don't feel very good right now." Maybe you actually said the word *no*. But I will bet you said it with a sheepish smile on your face and your eyes averted from his. News flash! You're trying to say no but your smile is saying yes. Guess which one of those two types of communication a man is getting? He thinks you are being coy. He definitely hears you saying yes to everything he is asking. So, while you are learning how to say no, no smiles.

Practice Dating

Dating is where you get to practice assertiveness, boundaries, and saying no. The more you date (and I mean "date," not have sex with, move in with, loan money to, hang out at your place, babysit his kids, have him babysit your kids, or loan him your car), the better you will become at recognizing those old feelings that led you to an abuser. Hopefully, after recognizing them, you will set firmer boundaries for yourself and end any budding relationship that begins to feel the same as your past abusive ones. And how do you end it, you ask? You speak honestly and clearly state your reason for no longer wanting to date him. If you identified abusive behavior, tell him exactly what he did that was unacceptable. Of course, he will have some reason for his behavior and insist that he is not really the way he seems. Too late. Say clearly you do not date people who treat you badly, the behavior was unacceptable, and you will not be seeing him again. I know, I know, you don't want to "hurt his feelings." If those are your thoughts, you are close, very close, to sliding back into the ugly abyss. Let's review. It is not your job to take care of other people's feelings. The men you date should be adults and as such they are responsible for managing their own feelings. If your date tries to induce those old guilty feelings, that's a huge red flag. Get away quick! If he tries to engage in a conversation that sounds anywhere close to the scenario presented earlier in this chapter, again, say, "No, I will not go out with you again." If he persists, simply say no and then leave. If you are out and you came in his car, call a friend or a cab to come get you. Never put yourself in a position where you are dependent on a date to get you home. Have a back up plan. Remember, this is practice. Think ahead about all possibilities. Dating is about getting to know a person. You don't know enough about a date, even after several months of good behavior, to know how he will react when you set boundaries and say no. And you can't rely on your past choices of men as an indication of how a person should behave. You are starting from scratch.

As you continue to practice dating, it will become easier and easier to say no without explanation because you will feel more in control each time you do. And when you respect yourself, you will respect others by not purposely choosing someone who is "less than" in order for you to feel needed and "better than."

How to Know When You are Healthy

Another aspect of practice dating occurs when you've been asked out by a truly healthy individual who is independent, has his own boundaries, speaks honestly, and has absolutely no need to be propped up by you. How you react to a person like this will depend on where you are in your process of achieving emotional independence. If you have not learned to truly love yourself and you still look to others to validate you, a healthy man is not going to be attractive to you. Your interaction with him is going to feel bland because you will be waiting to experience that familiar feeling of emotional intensity, the sugar rush. If you find yourself longing for him to tell you how beautiful you are, how he needs you, how sexy you are, and so on, you are not ready to date, not even practice dating. Yes, it's nice to get compliments, but needing them is not healthy. When *you* believe you are beautiful, intelligent, important, sexy, or whatever you think is important about yourself, you will not be waiting to hear the words from someone else. And if you indeed do not think of yourself in the terms that are important to you, then it is time to get busy and become the person you love. Return to your dream list and make yourself the person you want to be. I cannot emphasize enough that it is up to you. You have to *do* the things necessary to improve your self image. It is not enough to simply *say* you believe you have the qualities you desire. If you insist on remaining dependent on another person's opinions in order to feel good about yourself, you will continue to choose abusive partners. Unhealthy men will be the only ones attracted to you because you too will be unhealthy.

When your thoughts, feelings, and behavior are all in healthy accord, and you know the difference between *want* and *need*, then you should do well in your choice of men. You will want, not need, someone in your life, but not just anyone. You will choose someone who has the same qualities you have and who does not need you in his life, but instead wants you, chooses you. What a difference!

You will know you are healthy and have healed your lonely childhood when you can honestly say, "Today I *choose* to have this person in my life. I choose him because he is decent, kind, loving, intelligent, hardworking (fill in the healthy qualities you admire) ... I am with him because I want to be, not because I need him to give me compliments in order to feel okay about myself. Most importantly, I do not need him to keep me from feeling lonely. I am strong. I am capable. I can live alone. I can feel lonely and transform loneliness into love for myself. I am no longer a child and I will not die if I am not loved by someone else. I am free."

19

Making Peace with Mom, Dad, and the Tiger

In order to truly heal from your birth trauma of invisibility, you have to make peace with your mother (your father too, but primarily your mother). This person is the cause of your loneliness, so this is where you must go to resolve it. However, I am not saying you have to allow your parents back into your life if you have removed them and have decided it would be detrimental to reengage with them. What I am saying is there needs to be an acceptance of reality. Now that you have gained understanding of your life and why you chose the abusive men, you may be wondering why your mother or father did this to you. You understand *how* your situation evolved and now you want to know *why*. You may be thinking of informing your parents about your enlightenment and believe if they realize what they have done, they can fix it and all will be well. You will finally get the love you needed (past tense, since you are beyond that now) from them. Then you wouldn't be angry, hurt, and resentful anymore. Then you could go to your emotional home, a place of unconditional love and welcoming. Instead, you will end up going to the 7-Eleven mini-mart.

You are probably familiar with 7-Elevens or a similar convenience store. Those places that stay open all night and sell various items that people think they need at 2:00 AM. I would like you to picture one such place in your head and imagine yourself walking in the front door and approaching the clerk behind the counter. You walk up to

The Saber-Toothed Tiger

the clerk and say, "I'd like a steak, medium rare, a baked potato with sour cream and chives, and a Caesar salad on the side. Oh, and a small glass of red wine." The clerk gives you a strange look and replies, "Ah, lady, we don't have any of that, but you can go in the back. There're some hot dogs and nachos, and you can get a beer out of the cooler." That is not what you want to hear, so you repeat your request with a little more emphasis this time. Again, the clerk says with even more confusion, "Lady, we ain't got any of that, but you can get a wrapped sandwich, some chips, and a beer." Now the clerk is getting a little perturbed. But you are not satisfied and begin to demand in your sternest voice, "I want a steak, medium rare, a Caesar salad, a baked potato, and a glass of wine and I want it *now!*" Realistically, do you think you will ever get a steak dinner at 7-Eleven? That's right, you won't. Not because the clerk doesn't *want* to give it to you, but because he doesn't *have* it to give.

Your parents are like the 7-Eleven. If they'd had the love to give, they would have. Most parents try their best to be good parents. Some are overwhelmed with financial difficulties or physical or mental health problems. Some are struggling with addictions. Some parents are burned out from caretaking too many children. Some simply do not have the mental or emotional capacity to parent in a healthy way. Some may still be trying to resolve their feelings about the abuse or neglect they received as children from their own parents. Regardless of the reasons, no amount of demanding on your part will get you what they never had to give. You can pound on that door for the rest of your life, but there will be no answer.

If you wish to have a relationship with your parents, you will have to become an adult and have an adult-to-adult relationship with them. Your parents are no longer the big people who should know everything. They are fallible human beings, some greatly flawed. You are not that needy, lonely child begging for love anymore. From now on you will talk to your parents as an adult, setting boundaries, saying no, and speaking the truth, but not in a hurtful or vengeful way. Getting even is for children. I am not saying the treatment you received from your parents was sufficient. I am asking you to accept reality—they can't give what they don't have. Accept the reality that the only type of love you are ever going to get from your parents will be the oatmeal variety. You are an adult now, you can live with that. Your parents are not your emotional home. You must find your emotional home within the safety of your own heart.

There are religious and social proscriptions to "honor your mother and father." People get confused about this part of growing up. If you were abused by your parents or so neglected that your life was in danger, or if you were removed from your home and spent years in foster care, you might wonder how you are to honor when you are so angry and hurt. My answer to the dilemma is this: your parents gave you the greatest gift, the gift of life. For that you owe them. No, you don't owe them respect, money, affection, love, communication, or to be at their bedside when they die. You do not have to *love* your parents. Every act does not have to derive from love. You can act out of self-respect, obligation, or from your own sense of wanting to be a decent human being and overcome your beginnings. If your belief is that you do need to honor your parents, then the way you accomplish that is to honor the precious life they gave you. Honor your life by loving yourself, treating yourself well, not allowing others to hurt you, being assertive, and following your dreams. Honor your parents by honoring your own life.

When you love and honor yourself and your experience of invisibility and loneliness, and when you determine to live

The Saber-Toothed Tiger

your own life, you will be the strongest person you know. The Saber-Toothed Tiger, loneliness, will no longer be your enemy. You will tame him, share the cave, and sleep peacefully by the same fire.

> Call it loneliness,
> That deep, beautiful color
> No one can describe ...
> —Priest Jakuren
> *Only Companion: Japanese Poems of Love and Longing*

References

Angelou, Maya. 2001. Hallmark Cards, Inc.

Bandura, Albert. 1995. "Exercise of personal and collective efficacy in changing societies" in *Self-Efficacy in Changing Societies*, Albert Bandura, ed. New York: Cambridge University Press, 1–45.

Barnett, O., C. Miller-Perrin, and R. Perrin. 2005. *Family Violence Across the Lifespan, An Introduction* (2nd ed.). Thousand Oaks, CA: Sage Publications.

Chibucos, Thomas R., Randall W. Leite, with David L. Weis. *Readings in Family Theory*. 2005. Thousand Oaks, CA: Sage Publications.

Erlich, H. S. 1998. "On loneliness, narcissism, and intimacy." *The American Journal of Psycholanalysis* 58, no. 2: 135–162.

Feinberg, Cara. 2007. "Hitting Home." In *Annual Editions The Family 07/08*, Kathleen Gilbert, 146–150. Dubuque, IA.: McGraw-Hill Contemporary Learning Series.

First, Michael B., ed. 2000. *Diagnostic and Statistical Manual of Mental Disorders-IV TR*. 4th ed. Washington, DC: American Psychiatric Association.

Freud, Sigmund. 1938. "The Basic Writings of Sigmund Freud." Trans. A.A. Brill, New York: Random House.

Fromm, Erich. 1956. *The Art of Loving*. New York: Bantam Books, Inc.

Fry, P. S., and L A. Barker. 2002. "Quality of Relationships and Structural Properties of Social Support Networks of Female Survivors of Abuse." *Genetic, Social, and General Psychology Monographs* 128, no. 2: 139–163.

Gottman, John, and Joan DeClaire. 2001. *The Relationship Cure*. New York: Three Rivers Press.

Hamill, Sam, trans. 1992. *Only Companion, Japanese Poems of Love and Longing*. Boston: Shambhala Publications, Inc.

Hines, Denise, and Kathleen Malley-Morrison. 2005. *Family Violence in the United States: Defining, Understanding, and Combating Abuse*. Thousand Oaks, CA: Sage Publications.

Ihinger-Tallman, M., and T. Cooney. 2005. *Families in Context: An Introduction*. Los Angeles, CA: Rosbury Publishing Co.

Illinois State Museum. 2008. "Saber-toothed cats." www.museum.state.il.us/exhibits/larson/smilodon.html (18 February 2008).

Jacobson, Neil and John Gottman. 1998. *When Men Batter Women*. New York: Simon and Schuster.

Jung, Carl. 1971. In *The Portable Jung*, J Campbell, ed. New York: Viking Penguin, Inc.

Karraker, Meg W., and Janet R. Grochowski. 2006. *Families With Futures: A Survey of Family Studies for the*

Twenty-first Century. New Jersey: Lawrence Erlbaum Associates Inc., Publishers.

Kaiser, David A. January 2006. "The Science of Love: A Biography of Harry Harlow." *International Society for Neuronal Regulation Newsletter*, 10–13.

Lauer, R., and J. Lauer. 2007. *Marriage & Family* (6th ed.). New York: McGraw-Hill.

Muir, Darwin, and Kang Lee. 2003. "The Still-Face Effect: Methodological Issues and New Applications." *Infancy* 4, no. 4: 483–491.

Overmier, J. B., and M. E. P. Seligman. 1967. "Effects of inescapable shock upon subsequent escape and avoidance learning." *Journal of Comparative and Physiological Psychology* 63: 28–33.

Pence, Ellen, and Michael Paymar. 1993. *Education Groups for Men Who Batter: The Duluth Model*. New York: Springer Publishing Co.

Price, S., P. McKenry, and M. Murphy. 2000. *Families Across Time, A Life Course Perspective*. Los Angeles, CA: Roxbury Publishing Co.

Shaw, C. A. 2005. "The Sabertoothed Cats." In *Rancho La Brea; Death Trap and Treasure Trove*, J. M. Harris, 26–27. Los Angeles, CA: Natural History Museum.

Simons, R., L. Simons, and L. Wallace. 2004. *Families, Delinquency, and Crime: Linking Society's Most Basic Institution to Antisocial Behavior*. Los Angeles, CA: Roxbury Publishing Co.

Stiano, Tricia. 2004. "Direction of Regard and the Still-Face Effect in the First Year: Does Intention Matter?" *Child Development* 75, no. 2: 468–479.

Straus, Murray A., Richard J. Gelles, and Suzanne K. Steinmetz. 1980. *Behind Closed Doors, Violence in the American Family*. Garden City, N.Y.: Anchor Press/Doubleday.

Tronick, Edward Z. 1989. "Emotions and Emotional Communication in Infants." *American Psychologist* 44, no. 2: 112–119.

Tronick, E. Z. 2003. "Things Still to be Done on the Still-Face Effect." *Infancy* 4, no. 4: 475–482.

Tronick, E., A. Heidelise, L. Adamson, S. Wise, and B. Brazelton. 1978. "The Infant's Response to Entrapment between Contradictory Messages in Face-to-Face Interaction." *Journal of the American Academy of Child Psychiatry* 17, no. 1: 1–13.

University of California. 2008) "What Is a Sabertooth." www.ucm/berkeley.edu/mammal/carnivora/sabretooth.html (18 February 2008).

Walker, Lenore. 1979. *The Battered Woman*. New York: Harper & Row.

Zubretsky, Theresa M., and Karla M. Digirolamo. 1996. "The False Connection Between Adult Domestic Violence and Alcohol."

www.opdv.state.ny.us/health_humsvc/substance/falsecx.html.

LaVergne, TN USA
18 May 2010
183105LV00005B/7/P